Integrated Library Planning

A New Model for Strategic and Dynamic Planning, Management, and Assessment

Myka Kennedy Stephens

Association of College and Research Libraries
A division of the American Library Association | Chicago, Illinois 2023

The paper used in this publication meets the minimum requirements of American National Standard for Information Sciences–Permanence of Paper for Printed Library Materials, ANSI Z39.48-1992. ∞

Library of Congress Control Number: 2023935834

Copyright © 2023 by Myka Kennedy Stephens
Cover image created by Cecily Stephens

All rights reserved except those which may be granted by Sections 107 and 108 of the Copyright Revision Act of 1976.

Printed in the United States of America.

27 26 25 24 23 5 4 3 2 1

Contents

v   Introduction

1   Chapter 1. Infinite Horizons

15   Chapter 2. Pivoting Toward an Integrated Future

27   Chapter 3. Foundation and Groundwork

51   Chapter 4. Building a Planning Structure

75   Chapter 5. Implementing a Monthly Review Cycle

95   Chapter 6. Long-Term Assessment and Adjustment

117   Chapter 7. Stepping into an Integrated Future

129   Acknowledgments

133   Appendix A. Helpful Resources and Tools

139   Appendix B. Sample Report Outlines

143   Bibliography

145   About the Author

Introduction

Planning, strategic and otherwise, may evoke a variety of memories and raw emotions. It may stir excitement and anticipation, or perhaps a previous trauma. Take a moment to recall the last time you participated in a brainstorming session or other collaborative discussion intended to inform a planning process. Perhaps it was an all-day planning retreat with your colleagues, where you spent time writing down various challenges and threats along with thoughts and ideas to address them. Multicolored sticky notes littered the walls of the meeting room, along with larger sheets of paper containing the thoughts and wisdom of the room. At its best, the moment was perhaps filled with hope, excitement, and energy. At its worst, the moment might have been filled with skepticism, doubt, and emptiness. At its most deplorable, the moment left you feeling voiceless, dismissed, and marginalized.

What happened to the wisdom collected in that room on all those sticky notes? Hopefully, it was bundled up carefully by the leaders of the process to be further studied and thoughtfully considered. How much massaging and cleaning did those notes undergo to be transformed into an organized and neatly written document? The finished product might have borne little resemblance to the rainbow collection of notes from the walls of the meeting room and the raw thought they contained. When you read the document, perhaps you found a glimmer of the energy you remember from that day. Or perhaps you found your voice sterilized, pushed to the edge, or missing altogether. Regardless of the outcome, there is a truth: our past experiences with plans and planning practices influence how we engage with them.

I have a confession: I am a hopeless planner. It is a behavior that was instilled in me at a young age by my mother. I got my first datebook planner when I entered middle school and tracked everything in it from my homework assignments to the money I spent on a drink to go with my bag lunch. By the time I was in college, pocket-sized electronic planners were more affordable and became my device of choice for tracking appointments and storing notes (at least until the advent of the smartphone). Every project, every hobby, every vacation, every holiday meal has a plan. This prompts me to share another confession: my plans almost always change. I used to think that it was because I was always overly optimistic about the time it would take to finish tasks. With age and maturity, I now realize that my plans change because life changes. I learn new things, observe that something is not working right, or find help from an unexpected quarter. All of this gets incorporated into the plan as it is in process, enriching it as I progress toward my goal. By the time the plan reaches its conclusion, it looks much different from when I started and my finished product is usually successful. This is okay. In fact, it is better than okay. This is a good thing.

Over my twenty-year career in libraries, I have led or participated in several planning processes from small project plans to institution-wide strategic planning committees. Most of those processes followed a linear trajectory that involved creating the plan, doing the plan, and then reviewing the outcome of the plan. While this is a generalization and simplification of what can often be a complex, years-long endeavor in the case of institutional strategic plans, let us step back and look at the strict linear nature of this routine. Any new information that emerges during the "doing" of the plan may or may not be attended to. Depending on what kind of information it is and the level of urgency it presents, a plan might proceed with a slight change if it can remain on the same schedule or very close to it. If the new information is catastrophic in nature, the plan could be paused, halted, or discontinued. More often than not, however, the new information is potentially just disruptive enough to push a plan off schedule if allowed, so the planner sets it aside in a special holding place until the plan is complete in order to be incorporated in the next iteration. When the time comes to finally consider the new information, it is not new anymore and any opportunity that might have existed is now greatly diminished.

I have also been involved in planning processes that have felt forced, scripted, and predetermined. In other words, fake. An example of this kind of process is being asked to provide feedback on drafted goals and outcomes, sending in substantive feedback and participating in a facilitated group discussion that revises the goals and outcomes, only to see the final published report with the original goals and outcomes. Another scenario is being invited to bring fresh new ideas to a meeting only to have all the new ideas rejected and a variation on old ideas adopted instead. When this happens too many times, people stop offering their honest opinions and new ideas because they have learned that the planners do not really want to hear them. At this point, the organization has much bigger problems than their strategic plan.

As a hopeless planner, I believe in the power of planning. The act of setting goals and organizing the tasks needed to achieve these goals is life-giving for me. It helps me to visualize how I can accomplish my goals and achieve almost anything. However, in those moments when voices are silenced in favor of a prewritten outcome, or new information is set aside to be dealt with when the planning cycle is ready to repeat, I experience a frustration so deep that something withers inside me. Planning on the scale needed for an organization ought to be more like the best of planning on an individual scale: adaptable, flexible, responsive, and dynamic. How did our organizations and libraries get to such a rigid and unhealthy place with planning? How can we get them out of it?

Integrated Library Planning is a different kind of approach to planning that is both strategic and dynamic. It is fueled by open communication, honest assessment, and astute observation. Voices at the table, near the table, and far from the table are heard and considered. Its perpetual rhythm gives space to consider new information when it emerges and freedom to make changes at a time that makes sense instead of when it is most convenient or expected. The components of the model described on these pages might look deceptively similar to the strategic planning practices used in libraries and organizations for decades. Yet when implemented as a whole, with a monthly review cycle on a rolling planning horizon and space for regular analysis of information needs and behavior, it has the potential to shatter any previous notions of planning as a pointless waste of time serving only to satisfy administrators. Integrated Library Planning helps libraries effectively navigate and become agents of change.

Libraries were already well into a period of rapid change when I began developing Integrated Library Planning. I initially intended to complete this book after four years of fieldwork and writing. This book is now complete after eight years of fieldwork and writing—another example of needing to adapt one of my plans because life changes. I did not anticipate the dramatic shifts that are occurring as the result of COVID-19 and social reckoning over racism.

The nature of social change and the ways in which libraries are responding to it has shifted substantially in recent years. A case in point is a comparison of the rhetoric between the 2015 and 2021 ACRL environmental scans. In 2015, the ACRL Planning and Review Committee highlighted the rapid pace of change happening around libraries. This suggested a perception of change as something happening in the environment, something that libraries would find challenging. By 2021, COVID-19 and social issues forced higher education institutions and libraries to change whether they wanted it or were prepared for it. Change is no longer something that exists in the environment around our libraries; it is a way of being for our libraries, our parent institutions and organizations, and our local and global communities.

In these intervening years, as I have worked toward finishing this book, the value of and need for Integrated Library Planning has become clearer. The era of fixed-length strategic plans is coming to an end. Five-year strategic plans had already given way to three-year strategic plans, and now we find ourselves needing to plan and function when nothing is certain beyond the present moment. To shorten a fixed planning cycle using the same strategic planning tools and templates would be maddening, forcing planners to begin working on the next iteration when the current plan was barely launched. A perpetual, integrated planning model makes more sense in our present reality.

Overview and Outcomes

This book is an introduction to Integrated Library Planning. This model utilizes a rolling planning horizon and integrates cyclical evaluation and assessment, financial reconciliation, and strategic planning. The result is a responsive and dynamic approach to library leadership in which emerging needs and new trends are identified and proactively addressed. It is a model of planning designed for the current age of libraries, a time when constant ripples of change are accompanied by shockwaves of uncertainty. What has become especially clear in the wake of the COVID-19 pandemic is that libraries need to know as much as possible about their environments and communities so that informed decisions can be made in a timely and efficient manner, even quickly when necessary. Putting energy into three-year and five-year plans when the current year's budget is subject to sudden and unanticipated change is no longer a good use of our time and energy. This is especially the case as resources such as staff time are dwindling and becoming increasingly scarce in an over-stressed labor market. It is past time to shift to a new approach to planning, one that helps library leaders gain perspective on what their libraries do, discover what their patrons need most, and respond to crises and emerging needs flexibly, strategically, and smartly. I believe Integrated Library Planning is what libraries need to thrive in our ever-changing world.

The seven chapters in this book are a trail guide to implementing Integrated Library Planning and developing an integrated plan. Although I write from a location in a theological library—which I experience as a hybrid between an academic library and a special library with some public library sensibilities sprinkled in—this book is written to be accessible to a range of librarians and library leaders in a variety of contexts. Integrated Library Planning can be adapted to fit any size library, with any type of organizational structure, in any kind of context. It can complement existing strategic plans imposed on libraries by their parent organizations, and it can also incorporate external review and assessment cycles to reduce duplication of work. I hope that whatever your library's history, context, or present planning needs are, you will find a resonance with what this book has to offer.

Chapter 1 explores the philosophical and theoretical ideas that form the foundation of Integrated Library Planning. It explores the realities of change, the different ways it can be defined, and how we might respond to it and live with it. This chapter defines Integrated Library Planning and the five core components that keep a plan moving forward: the rolling planning horizon, engagement with the library's identity, intentional organizational structure, ongoing observation, and cyclical assessments. It also provides a brief overview of the four stages of the Integrated Library Planning process.

Chapter 2 sits with the reader at the point of decision-making. Deciding to depart from previous planning practices and engage in a new model of planning is a big step for any library. This chapter looks at three areas a library leader may want to examine before starting the Integrated Library Planning process. First, it is important to determine how well a library might pivot toward an integrated plan. Second, library leaders will want to share the concept of Integrated Library Planning carefully and intentionally with stakeholders, assembling feedback and answering any questions that arise, before starting the process. Third, it is helpful to thoroughly research the model and the various tools and methods it employs and think ahead to who will be involved in the planning process, so that everyone is well prepared once the development timeline begins.

The first stage of Integrated Library Planning, foundation and groundwork, is introduced in chapter 3. This is the initial research phase for the plan and can last six to twelve months. The planning team gathers background information about the library, its parent organization, and the surrounding community. Mission and vision statements are also drafted and vetted during this stage. The planning team conducts a comprehensive needs assessment, which includes statistical research (quantitative), collecting surveys and feedback (mixed methods), and hosting conversations (qualitative). The final research tool is a SWOT matrix, which synthesizes the findings from all the various research activities. These research activities are not intended to be strictly linear. As the planning team learns from its research, it may find new questions to ask, additional background information to locate, and revisions to make to the mission and vision statements.

The second stage of Integrated Library Planning, building the planning structure, is described fully in chapter 4. The planning structure has four levels. The base level is the library's organizational structure, described as operational areas. These operational areas may also be organized into divisions or departments if the planning team finds it helpful. Stemming from each operational area are the goals. Goals are written specifically for each operational area and relate to the library's mission and vision statements. Stemming from the goals are strategic outcomes. While a goal is usually an ideal state of being for the operational area, a strategic outcome is realistically achievable and may even have a timeframe assigned to it. Each strategic outcome has individual action plans. This is the level that gets mapped onto the rolling planning horizon and tracked for completion.

Chapter 5 covers the third stage of Integrated Library Planning, which begins to shift from development into implementation. In the third stage, the monthly review cycle is created and implemented. The monthly review cycle has three functions: to facilitate communication about what is going on in and around the library, to provide an opportunity for assessment, and to support planning that incorporates what is learned through communication and assessment. The product of the monthly review cycle is a monthly review report, which includes progress assessments, a current financial summary, an analysis of observed information needs and behavior, and a summary of updates to the integrated plan. It is important to develop a monthly review cycle that is sustainable for the library. This chapter offers several suggestions on how it may be customized for a variety of libraries based on size, staffing models, and institutional relationships.

Once a monthly review cycle is implemented, an integrated plan matures into the fourth stage: long-term assessment and adjustment. Chapter 6 covers how a library staff begins to live and work with an integrated plan, open to revision and adjustment throughout its implementation. As library staff observe information behavior, strategic responses may be woven into the plan. Regular financial review and reconciliation can inform decision making as new needs and opportunities emerge. Planning on a rolling horizon and adding action plans to it as they are developed encourages the practices of setting and resetting priorities and creating space for new initiatives. Integrated Library Planning and the monthly review cycle are designed to prompt regular reflection on the foundations of the plan: the mission and vision statements, goals, and strategic outcomes. Therefore, a mature integrated plan allows library leaders to revise goals and strategic outcomes, perhaps even revisiting some of the exercises and processes that went into the development of the plan, so that the plan remains relevant, current, and forward-facing. This chapter also explores how a mature integrated plan might incorporate external review cycles.

Chapter 7 closes the book with some reflections on what leading a library through Integrated Library Planning brings to the library, the library's staff, and the communities it serves. It explores the importance of balancing the work of assessment with observation and analysis. A library will encounter inevitable challenges with an integrated plan, as with any plan. These challenges can be overcome, and they are also learning experiences that help make the integrated plan stronger. The perpetual movement of the rolling planning horizon carries a lot of forward momentum that can sweep up a library and its staff. When this happens, it is important to pause, take stock of what has been achieved, and celebrate the accomplishments.

My hope is that readers will finish this book with an understanding of Integrated Library Planning and confidence to try it in their library. Readers will find their libraries represented in the many examples and case studies and see the possibilities and opportunities that an integrated plan can awaken for a library. For readers who are burned-out on strategic plans that seem more decorative than functional, this book may offer renewal and a fresh approach to planning that can be dynamic, responsive, and relevant. Above all, I aim to equip and empower readers to lead their libraries *responsively* instead of *reactively*, with healthy curiosity, shrewd rationality, and effervescent creativity, and with sensibilities that are grounded in the present while looking toward the future.

A Note about Names

While this is my first single-author book, I have published articles and presented widely about my experiences with Integrated Library Planning, hosting conversations in the library, adopting open-source software solutions, and more. Many of those publications reference my work at Schaff Library, Lancaster Theological Seminary while this book references my work at Lancaster Theological Seminary Library. Philip Schaff's name was removed from the library and library building in February 2020 by a vote of the seminary's trustees following an investigation into the legacy of Schaff's writings on race. It was the first step in a long process that is underway at Lancaster Theological Seminary to be transparent about and share our complicated history and to address the systemic racism that is still present in our communities.

This book includes several case studies that illustrate a particular method or practice. The libraries and scenarios in these case studies are all fictitious. I chose to name the libraries in these case studies after noted civil rights activists and leaders out of respect for their contributions to society and in acknowledgement of the fact that there is still much more to be done to dismantle white privilege, make reparations for the horrors of slavery, and advance true racial equality in the United States and beyond. The following civil rights leaders are eponymized in these case studies:

Mary White Ovington (1865–1951) was co-founder of the National Association for the Advancement of Colored People (NAACP). She was also a suffragist and advocated for women's right to vote in the United States.

Carter G. Woodson (1875–1950) was founder of the Association for the Study of African American Life and History and pioneered the celebration of Negro History Week, the precursor to Black History Month. He was a scholar of American history, especially African American history, earned a PhD from Harvard University, and served as Dean of the College of Arts and Sciences at Howard University.

Rosa Parks (1913–2005) is best known for her defiant act of civil disobedience on a public bus in Montgomery, AL, refusing to give up her seat to a white person. She was a civil rights activist throughout her life and was awarded the Presidential Medal of Freedom in 1996.

W. E. B. Du Bois (1868–1963) was a co-founder of the NAACP. He was an American sociologist, was the first African American to earn a PhD from Harvard University, and was a professor of history, sociology, and economics at Atlanta University.

Medgar Evers (1925–1963) was a civil rights activist who helped to overturn segregation at the University of Mississippi. He was a WWII Army veteran who actively sought to dismantle segregation and expand opportunities for African Americans.

Elizabeth Freeman (c. 1744–1829) was the first enslaved African American to file and win a legal suit for her freedom. As a free woman, she became known for her skills as a healer, midwife, and nurse.

Fred Shuttlesworth (1922–2011) was a co-founder of the Southern Christian Leadership Conference. He was a Baptist pastor who led efforts to dismantle segregation and other forms of racism in Birmingham, AL.

Charles Hamilton Houston (1895–1950) was the first special counsel to the NAACP and argued several important civil rights cases before the US Supreme Court. He also served as Dean of Howard University Law School.

Josephine St. Pierre Ruffin (1842–1924) was editor and publisher of *Women's Era*, the first national newspaper by and for African American women. She actively supported women's suffrage, was a charter member of the NAACP, and co-founded the League of Women for Community Service.

Martin Luther King, Jr. (1929–1968) was the most visible leader in the US civil rights movement. His activism was inspired by his Christian beliefs and the nonviolent philosophies of Mahatma Gandhi. He was a Baptist pastor and one of the leaders of the 1963 March on Washington.

John Lewis (1940–2020) was the chairman of the Student Nonviolent Coordinating Committee from 1963 to 1966 and led several marches from Selma to Montgomery, including the one that became known as Bloody Sunday. He later served as a US congressman representing the fifth congressional district of Georgia for seventeen terms.

Harriet Tubman (c. 1822–1913) escaped slavery and subsequently led missions to rescue enslaved people, establishing a network of antislavery activists and safe houses that became known as the Underground Railroad. She also worked for the Union Army during the US Civil War and was an active suffragist.

Thurgood Marshall (1908–1993) founded the NAACP Legal Defense and Educational Fund and successfully argued several civil rights cases before the US Supreme Court, including *Brown v. Board of Education*. He was the first African American to serve as a US Supreme Court justice.

CHAPTER 1

Infinite Horizons

Libraries occupy a unique place in our society. They are repositories of knowledge acquired through centuries of experience and exploration. They are also openly available access points for that knowledge and information. As the ways in which we communicate as a society and as individuals change and the ways in which we access and acquire knowledge change, libraries are called upon to change as well. It is a strange yet natural charge: to be held responsible for the preservation of centuries-old information while simultaneously exploring new technologies that support universal access to that information.

When I became the chief administrator of a small, specialized academic library, I quickly realized that if I focused solely on meeting the needs of the library and its patrons as I was able to perceive them in the moment, I would forever be one step behind. For example, designing and implementing a new library service to meet needs based on data from a graduating student questionnaire might positively improve the experience of current students or it might not. Depending on what the service is and how long it takes to design and implement, there is a strong chance that the service would no longer be relevant at the time of its launch or would need updating almost immediately. This is particularly true of library services that integrate or rely upon information technology, including computers, mobile devices, and the internet. In an era when new devices are released on an annual schedule and software applications release updates every month or even every week, it becomes a matter of survival to be able to rapidly assess, navigate, and anticipate trends so as not to be left behind before really getting started.

A new kind of thinking is needed to lead libraries through times of transition and rapid change. Traditional approaches to strategic planning, project management, and assessment cycles are a fine place for libraries to start, but these approaches fail to withstand the rigorous challenges of our fast-paced, technology-driven society. To be successful in fulfilling my specialized academic library's mission, I needed to detect and understand the present needs of its users, to understand the present trends of similar libraries, and to develop the capacity to anticipate future needs and trends. I needed an approach that integrates ongoing research and observation with strategic planning and assessment, allowing me to plot an effective trajectory for developing the collection, creating relevant resources, and innovating timely library services.

This line of inquiry and exploration led me to develop a new model for library planning, management, and assessment that I call Integrated Library Planning. It is a dynamic and responsive process that equips librarians for forward-thinking leadership. As I explored ways to meet the challenges facing the library I administered, I realized that these challenges were not unique to specialized libraries and schools, nor even academic libraries and higher education. Transition and multifaceted change are a reality facing not-for-profits and community service organizations, businesses, and industries. Being able to understand and anticipate user needs is akin to market analysis and projection, a survival skill for many profit-driven businesses and corporations. Seeing the alignment of challenges across other industries and fields of practice, I drew on the work of leaders, planners, managers, and researchers from a variety of disciplines to make Integrated Library Planning a highly adaptable, flexible, and effective model for managing an information organization.

This chapter explores the philosophical underpinnings of Integrated Library Planning and what drives the process. Integrated Library Planning began as an adaptation of Integrated Business Planning, a corporate sector best practice. Overviews of this framework as well as other frameworks for strategic planning and assessment that inform Integrated Library Planning are also covered. It concludes with an outline of Integrated Library Planning, introducing the stages explored in depth throughout this book.

The Infinite Horizon and Planning Change

In the foundation of Integrated Library Planning are three main tenets. These ideas, or threshold concepts, encapsulate the philosophical foundation for this approach to organizational management and leadership. The goal is planning that is both strategic and dynamic. While my experience as a librarian helped to form them, these tenets are not exclusive to libraries and could be applied to almost any organization exploring strategically oriented integrated planning processes. They are

1. change is both a constant and a variable;

2. infinite potential comes from a planning horizon that rolls forward; and
3. proactive and responsive planning is a frequent, cyclical, inquiry-driven process.

Unpacking these tenets provides a glimpse into the thought processes that facilitate adopting an integrated planning model.

Change Is Both a Constant and a Variable

In mathematics and physics, a constant is something that is known and fixed in an equation. The speed of light, the Earth's gravitational pull, the number pi—these are all constants. No matter which formula or equation calls for these values, the same fixed value is always used to compute the answer. A variable is the opposite of a constant. It is an unknown value that could change based upon the other factors in the equation. Variables are often represented by the letter x, and the goal of solving an equation is often to find the value of that variable.

Since constants and variables are diametrically opposed, then it may seem paradoxical to claim that change is both. Yet, change is an ever-present force. Evidence for this is in weather patterns, the changing of seasons, and the aging process. Each day, in each moment, something in the Universe changes. Ongoing changes are often difficult to see and observe. They may go overlooked until a major event occurs and, then, when that moment passes into history, it becomes identified as a moment of change. In reality, even when major moments of change happen, they do not happen in isolation but are the result of ongoing and ever-present forces of change that are part of life.

Although change is an ever-present force in life, it often takes on different shapes and intensities. It ebbs and flows and moves in complex patterns that are difficult to predict. This is the variable nature of change. While it persists through every moment in time and is a factor in every event, its shape, size, intensity, and force of influence are all unknown. The variable nature of change makes it elusive and difficult to understand. It is the human tendency to simplify the forces of change into singular moments or a series of events that we commonly label as change. We do this in hindsight, appearing surprised or unprepared when faced with another moment of change.

To fully accept the dual nature of change as both constant and variable, we must increase our awareness and shift our mode of operation from control to interaction. Margaret Wheatley, in her groundbreaking book *Leadership and the New Science*, argues that using our innate capacity to adapt and work with change is far more effective than any effort to control or deny change. Change invites our curiosity, welcomes our questions, and feeds our imaginations. Simplifying it to a single moment or reducing it to a series of events diminishes its pervasiveness. It is not something that can or should be stopped, reversed, or mitigated. It is a force to acknowledge and a factor to work with.

Infinite Potential Comes from a Planning Horizon that Rolls Forward

When we shift our thinking about change and how we interact with it, the way we consider organizational planning and management also shifts. Standards and best practices across a wide variety of industries include some form of strategic planning. It is taught as part of management and leadership courses in business schools, library schools, and graduate schools of education, to name a few. While there are many variations on the strategic planning process, it typically follows this basic recipe: Background research and reflection on the organization's mission and vision are combined to lead to the development of goals, strategic outcomes, and action plans. The entire plan is fit into a fixed time frame called the planning horizon. It is most common to see planning horizons that span three to five years. Checkpoints, milestones, and targets may be added to the planning horizon to help determine if the plan is still on course or if it is running ahead of or behind schedule. When the plan reaches the end of its planning horizon, there is an evaluation and assessment period to review the actual outcomes against the goals and predicted outcomes of the plan. Since having an active strategic plan is an expectation and often a requirement, an organization will then repeat the process to establish revised goals and strategic outcomes that will be pursued over the course of a new fixed planning horizon.

While this is a very basic and rudimentary summary of strategic planning, consider what happens when the idea of working with the constant and variable nature of change is introduced into the planning process. During the beginning phase of strategic planning, a response to changes that are already known or predicted may be incorporated into the goals, strategic outcomes, and action plans. Once the strategic plan is in the implementation phase, however, additional unanticipated changes from both external and internal sources have little direct influence over the goals and outcomes, which have already been set and fixed into the planning horizon. Depending on the person leading the implementation of the strategic plan, there may be some flexibility and room for slight adjustment. Major realignment of goals and strategic outcomes, however, usually must wait until a strategic plan reaches the end of its life and enters the assessment phase. Meanwhile, strategic response to new changes that arose during the implementation of the plan is delayed, additional change may have occurred, and the organization may be caught a step behind its peers who were better positioned to respond to change. When viewed from this perspective, traditional approaches to strategic planning suddenly seem insufficient.

To make a shift toward a process that can incorporate changes as they occur, we must reconsider the planning horizon. A traditional planning horizon is a fixed length of time, giving the plan a lifespan. A horizon is a boundary, so the planning horizon establishes boundaries for a start and finish. However, our perception of the horizon that we observe in nature, dividing earth and sky, for example, does not work this way. It is always in the distance. When we travel further along a path, we never actually draw closer to the horizon because we still see it distantly in front of us.

Suppose we reconceive a planning horizon to reflect the qualities of the horizon we observe in nature. Determining a fixed distance between the organization and the edge of the planning horizon creates a planning horizon that begins to roll forward incrementally as the organization implements its plan. For every unit of time that passes during the plan's implementation, an equivalent unit of time is added to the end. As a result, the fixed and finite nature of the traditional planning horizon is reshaped into an infinitely rolling planning horizon. The capacity to work with change grows considerably when operating on a rolling horizon.

Proactive and Responsive Planning Is a Frequent, Cyclical, Inquiry-Driven Process

Making the shift from a fixed planning horizon to an infinitely rolling planning horizon is critical for acknowledging and working with the constant and variable forces of change that we encounter in every moment. Reconceiving the planning horizon invites us to reconsider the processes that result in an actual plan. While a traditional strategic planning process fits well with a fixed planning horizon, it would be awkward and difficult to map this same planning process onto a rolling horizon. Another shift is needed.

The purpose of a rolling horizon is to remove the fixed boundaries of time from the planning process in order to create space for exploring changes that occur while the plan is implemented. Exploring change with the intent to understand it and work with it demands a new, responsive process. A traditional strategic planning process creates space for this type of exploration at the beginning and at the end of the plan's life. By contrast, a rolling horizon invites a cyclical process occurring synchronously with its forward momentum. This cyclical process is shorter in duration, matching the unit of time marking the rolling horizon. This makes it possible to explore and engage changes more frequently, resulting in a dynamic plan that is capable of a timelier response by the organization to the needs of the community it serves.

A frequent, cyclical planning process on a rolling horizon must be inquiry-driven to remain strategically focused as well as proactive and responsive. This inquiry involves an ongoing examination of how change impacts the organization and its mission. Planning that is strategic, proactive, and responsive must perpetually engage and evaluate the organization's mission and vision, along with its stated goals and outcomes. As the plan moves forward, new knowledge may be incorporated as it surfaces, expanding the capacity of an organization to innovate.

When embraced together, these three tenets offer a new approach to strategic planning. It is an approach that offers space to be curious about change and an opportunity to integrate new ideas and knowledge at the precise moment when it is most appropriate. Libraries carry tremendous potential. Tapping that potential requires finding a way to navigate a sea of transitions and to innovate alongside and in conversation with the many changes that are occurring. Exploring and understanding these tenets and implementing an Integrated Library Planning process has the power to turn a jumble of transitions and potential into a transformative leadership opportunity.

Integrated Library Planning Defined

Integrated Library Planning is a model that librarians may use to better understand, plan, and act on change. It integrates ongoing review and assessment with the development and achievement of goals and outcomes. It features a rolling horizon for mapping action plans and a monthly review cycle that promotes communication and collaboration across the library. The way in which I have implemented Integrated Library Planning in my library draws on a variety of theories, concepts, and tools developed by thinkers in the fields of leadership, strategic planning, and information studies. These are theories, concepts, and tools that resonate with me, with how I perceive librarianship and library leadership, and with how I function as a library director. There is room in the model for other theories, concepts, and tools. It is not necessarily exclusive to one school of thought and is adaptable and open to interpretation.

An Inspired Model

Integrated Library Planning integrates all aspects of library operation into one perpetual assessment, planning, and evaluation process. The inspiration comes from Integrated Business Planning (IBP), an offshoot of Sales & Operations Planning (S&OP). IBP is among corporate best practices for manufacturing and other businesses. It has been adopted by a wide range of global businesses because it fosters cooperation and coordination between departments, resulting in more efficient operation and strategic development of the business. Too often in large corporations, departments can be siloed. For example, the consumer research department might propose changes that may have adverse effects on production or may disrupt the supply chain. With IBP, the work of all departments is integrated under one plan and process, communicated clearly through departmental representatives on an executive team. New information that emerges from a consumer research department goes through an integrated reconciliation process as part of IBP to identify the most strategic responses and to determine how and when a response might fit into the business's plan.

Libraries are not corporations, though there are some similarities in how a library might approach planning. Libraries provide products in the form of collections and an array of services designed to provide and promote access to these collections. Libraries also experience demand in the form of circulation, reference inquiries, purchase suggestions, and more. There is also a tendency within libraries to become siloed. Libraries can be siloed both internally and externally, for example, when the work of technical services is not informed by data collected from reference interviews, or when the library is not represented or involved in decision-making by its parent institution. Integrated Library Planning is a model that provides libraries with an opportunity to open the lines of communication, become attuned to what is going on in all aspects of library operation, and integrate vision with data to form a clear strategic path responsive to the emerging needs and trends of the library's communities.

Ongoing Assessment-Informed Planning

Integrated Library Planning is an ongoing planning process. Once started, its cycle may continue for as long as the library finds it useful and productive. Five components prevent a library's integrated plan from becoming stale. In addition to the rolling planning horizon already discussed at the beginning of this chapter, the other components are identity, organizational structure, observation, and assessment.

The starting point and guiding star for the entire model is the library's discovery and development of its identity. How the library understands itself is the foundation for Integrated Library Planning. Who does the library serve? To what community or communities does it belong? What are the library's strengths and specialties? Is there anything notable or distinctive about the library, its building, its collections, its services, or its location? What are the library's values and how are they embodied? While the library begins to discover and articulate its identity during the initial stages of Integrated Library Planning, full implementation of an integrated plan allows a library's self-understanding to develop and evolve.

Development and implementation of an integrated plan also invites engagement with the library's organizational structure. Sometimes a library's organizational structures are too rigid, defined by roles established in another age. Integrated Library Planning uncovers the potential to restructure and form stronger connections between the library's identity and how it is embodied through the collaborative work of the library's staff. For larger libraries, this may be an opportunity to redefine departments or reconfigure the reporting structure that determines how library staff relate to one another. In smaller libraries, this may be an opportunity to evaluate each staff member's skills, interests, and talents to better match them with tasks that they find stimulating and fulfilling.

Staying attuned to what is going on within the library and around it feeds an integrated plan. Observation is a crucial skill in Integrated Library Planning. It involves collecting quantitative and qualitative data by showing how patrons are using the library, recording interactions with patrons, staying abreast of trends and developments in libraries and information technology, and regularly researching demographics and other data about the community the library serves. Observing everything that happens within the library and everything the library does with active curiosity creates a mindset that fosters creativity. Keeping senses alert feeds into the integrated plan, sparking new innovations that can be timely and efficiently implemented.

In tandem with the rolling planning horizon, ongoing assessment keeps an integrated plan moving forward. Similar to observation, it also feeds the integrated plan. While observation feeds the creative aspects of planning, assessment feeds the critical aspects. To perform assessment as part of an integrated plan is to critically engage with the library's operations. Is a particular task or action necessary? Does it add value—to the library, the community, the body of knowledge maintained by libraries? Does it meet a need? Could it be improved? Since Integrated Library Planning is an ongoing, perpetual planning process, inquiry-driven assessment is continual throughout the development and implementation of the plan. Unlike in traditional strategic planning where assessment might only be conducted at the end of the plan's timeline or at key milestones, Integrated Library Planning engages in assessment regularly and frequently as part of the monthly review cycle.

Flexible and Adaptable

As a model, Integrated Library Planning is flexible and adaptable, nimble enough to accommodate an array of tools, practices, and methods. The tools, practices, and methods described in this book are not definitive for developing and implementing an integrated plan. There are many other resources that might be utilized or incorporated into an integrated plan. This flexibility gives freedom to tailor the Integrated Library Planning process to fit any library's needs and offers unlimited options to revise and update implementation workflows as a library grows and changes. What I most hope for readers is that you may successfully incorporate practices and habits that resonate with you, from a wide range of planning tools and leadership philosophies, to make Integrated Library Planning something that works for you and your library.

One popular set of practices that might easily be incorporated into Integrated Library Planning is that of adaptive leadership. Based on the writings of Ronald Heifetz, Alexander Grashow, and Marty Linsky, adaptive leadership includes an array of tools and tactics that can fit into the Integrated Library Planning model. For example, the concept of "getting on the balcony" to get perspective on what is happening in an organization works beautifully with the assessment portions of Integrated Library Planning. Adaptive leadership also speaks to leaders of organizations who are experiencing change and transition. Integrated Library Planning is a model designed for libraries that are ready to embrace the rapid and widespread change that our industry and our communities continue to face since the advent of personal computers and the internet. Many of the habits and tactics described by Heifetz, Grashow, and Linsky help with developing and implementing an integrated plan. This makes adaptive leadership a prime example of a leadership philosophy with much to contribute to Integrated Library Planning.

While there is more than one leadership or planning philosophy that could be woven into an Integrated Library Planning process, this book tries not to ascribe fully to any one of these philosophies. Yes, Margaret Wheatley's philosophy and theory of self-organizing systems was one of my primary influences and inspirations and, yes, Integrated Business Planning (IBP) was the creative muse that prompted me to think of new ways of planning for libraries. Subsequent chapters will introduce practices such as hosting conversations and Appreciative Inquiry, along with tools like Gantt charts, to be used in an Integrated Library Planning process. I emphasize throughout this book that these are suggestions. These tools and practices are not required components of Integrated Library Planning. This is not a rigid model with limitations. Rather, Integrated Library Planning encourages incorporation and adaptation of tools and practices that make the most sense and resonate with the library developing and implementing the plan.

Integrated Library Planning is also a highly adaptable model for any type of library context. It is scalable for libraries of every size. It can also accommodate various staffing models and organizational structures. It was developed in a small academic library that serves members of the public and has a specialized collection focus, thus sharing some common ground with public libraries and special libraries. Adaptation has become a normal mode of operation for me in my experience as a library leader, therefore Integrated Library Planning is presented as an open model that welcomes and encourages adaptation. While its flexible and adaptable nature may make it difficult to define Integrated Library Planning, it makes it a stronger and more relevant model for libraries in the twenty-first century.

Overview of Integrated Library Planning

Preliminary: Pivoting toward an integrated future

Stage 1: Foundation and groundwork

Stage 2. Building a planning structure

Stage 3. Implementing a monthly review cycle

Stage 4. Long-term assessment and adjustment

Before starting any new plan, it is helpful to first examine the process for creating that plan. Taking time to discern, decide, and pivot toward a new planning approach is a preliminary step in the Integrated Library Planning process. Once a decision is made to try an integrated approach, library leaders embark on a four-stage development and implementation process. Progression through these stages is intended to be sequential and linear; however, Integrated Library Planning is a cyclical and iterative planning process. Practices that are engaged in the initial stages are revisited in later stages. Processes may be repeated and carried out multiple times within a stage. While it may seem like a straightforward, linear progression through these four stages, developing and implementing an integrated plan is actually a fluid process that can circle and flow through various practices as it matures.

The first stage involves foundational work for the plan. Gathering background information about your library and organization is the first step. This involves researching the institution's history and studying previous plans to determine what worked well and what did not. Next, give attention to the library's mission and vision statements. This is an opportunity to revise or rewrite them, or perhaps start fresh. This stage also includes the first needs assessment of the Integrated Library Planning process. Looking at statistics and usage patterns, conducting surveys and collecting feedback from patrons, and asking questions that open conversation about the future of the library are all practices that can be engaged in as part of the needs assessment in this first stage. The information collected in the needs assessment informs the development of a SWOT matrix—strengths, weaknesses, opportunities, and threats. Throughout this first stage, needs assessment and SWOT analysis may reveal the need for additional research of the library's history or a reconsideration of the mission and vision statements. When all these pieces are developed sufficiently to begin thinking about planning, it is time to move on to the second stage.

Building the planning structure is the focus of the second stage. It is important to note that this stage does not begin with jumping straight into planning, as one might be tempted to do. Rather it begins with the process of determining how the plan will be organized. Much of how an integrated plan is organized is determined by how the library's operations are organized. While a library may be content with how it is structurally organized, insights may have emerged from the first stage that prompt a reexamination of operations. Staff might need redeployment based on changing needs or perhaps a departmental structure that worked well two decades ago is no longer efficient. Establishing an optimal organizational structure for library operations then informs how the integrated plan will be structured. Now the planning work can begin. Goals and strategic outcomes are developed for each operational division and area within the library. These are the anchors for the work of the plan, the marks by which the plan will be measured. Goals and strategic outcomes do not have to be numerous to start with; one set for each operational area is a sufficient starting point. After crafting the goals and strategic outcomes, action plans are developed to populate the initial rolling horizon timeline for the integrated plan.

Having created goals, strategic outcomes, and a few preliminary action plans, the integrated plan moves from development to implementation during the third stage. Implementation of an integrated plan starts by establishing the rhythm of a monthly review cycle. The monthly review cycle involves communication, assessment, and planning. These three activities keep the plan moving forward as the rolling horizon inches forward with the passage of time. Communication keeps everyone informed about what is going on, the status of action plans, and progress toward completing strategic outcomes and fulfilling goals. Routine assessment includes data collection and analysis along with observed information behavior, which prompts reflection and opportunity to engage the elements of the integrated plan. Since the plan operates on a perpetually rolling horizon, the monthly review cycle also provides opportunity to establish the new planning horizon as the past month drops off and a future month is added. The companion to the monthly review cycle is a monthly review report, in which all the information from the cycle is collected and recorded. Establishing a monthly review cycle may take longer than one month to establish, so the third stage of Integrated Library Planning usually lasts several months while new workflows are established and navigated.

Once a library has made a smooth transition into the monthly review cycle, the integrated plan enters the fourth stage: long-term assessment and adjustment. This stage represents the maturation of the integrated plan. Practices and tools utilized during this stage encompass many of the activities carried out during the first three stages. As mentioned above for stage three, the assessment and planning practices in the monthly review cycle invite continual reflection on the effectiveness of the integrated plan in relation to what is actively happening in and around the library. When new opportunities or emerging needs arise during the monthly review cycle, there are processes within the cycle that support rescheduling action plans on the rolling horizon, revising strategic outcomes, rewriting goals, and a host of other adjustments. In a way, the hardest work of Integrated Library Planning takes place during this stage. When a library reaches this stage, it is ready to form strategic responses to observed information behavior recorded in the monthly review reports and is equipped to make effective decisions that keep its collections and services current and relevant to patrons. This fourth stage is not an end point or destination for an integrated plan; it is a touchstone for an engaged future of planning, assessment, and innovation integrated within the monthly review cycle.

Summary

There is an infinite horizon of possibility open to libraries and library leaders who explore Integrated Library Planning. It is a model of planning for those who seek to strategically respond to change instead of reacting to, ignoring, or postponing it. With every passing day, week, month, year, and decade, librarians continue to see evidence that change is both a constant and a variable. It is something that is with us always yet morphs into different shapes. Library leaders must provide space for change in strategic planning processes if libraries hope to remain responsive to what is going on in and around them. Integrated Library Planning achieves this with a rolling planning horizon and an inquiry-driven monthly review cycle.

Defined simply, Integrated Library Planning is a model that integrates processes for perpetual planning and assessment. It draws on regular financial review and collects observations of patron information behavior. The goal is to promote communication and collaboration across all areas of the library and between the library and its parent institution (school, civic community, organization). The outcome is a dynamic and responsive planning process that helps librarians to better understand, plan for, and act upon change. It was inspired by Integrated Business Planning (IBP) and is an ongoing planning process that does not have a static planning period or finite end date. The ongoing Integrated Library Planning process is fueled by the library's identity, organizational structure, a rolling planning horizon, observation, and assessment. It is a flexible and adaptable model. Many leadership theories and organizational philosophies are compatible with Integrated Library Planning, making this an open model for any library to adapt to fit their context.

There are four stages to Integrated Library Planning. The first stage opens with foundation and groundwork for starting development of an integrated plan. This includes a lot of research and analysis. The second stage continues with developing the structure that the integrated plan will use. The plan's structure is usually inherited from the library's organizational structure; therefore, this stage provides an opportunity to revisit how the library's operations are organized. The third stage shifts into implementation with the initiation of the monthly review cycle. This cycle and its companion report are the driving force behind Integrated Library Planning. There are several options for customizing the monthly review cycle and report to fit the library's context and purposes, so this stage may last several months as new the new integrated planning workflows take shape. The fourth stage represents the maturation of an integrated plan as the rhythms of the monthly review cycle take hold and attention shifts toward assessment and adjustment workflows that ensure the plan's long-term viability. It is at this point that the infinite horizon leads to a responsive, dynamic, and integrated future for the library, its staff, and its patrons.

Before beginning the first of these four stages, some important discernment and preparation must be done. Library leaders must first determine whether Integrated Library Planning is a good fit for what the library needs. Will it be supported by library staff and other stakeholders? Does the library have the capacity to pivot toward an integrated approach? This time of discernment and point of decision-making is the next topic.

- Preliminary: Pivoting toward an integrated future
- Stage 1: Foundation and groundwork
- Stage 2. Building a planning structure
- Stage 3. Implementing a monthly review cycle
- Stage 4. Long-term assessment and adjustment

CHAPTER 2

Pivoting Toward an Integrated Future

Choosing to adopt an Integrated Library Planning process and beginning the journey to develop an integrated plan is not a decision to be made quickly or lightly. Not only do you as a library leader need to be ready for the adventure, but the library also needs to be ready. Oftentimes, the plans and processes that successfully bring innovation occur at an almost magical time when conditions are right for both the organization leading the innovation and the environment around it that is ready to embrace change. Inherent within Integrated Library Planning are practices that help library leaders hone skills to detect what changes are occurring around and within the library, to innovate effectively within this changing environment, and to sense when the timing is appropriate to introduce new initiatives. A certain aptitude with some of these skills is also needed to determine the most appropriate time to begin an Integrated Library Planning process and how best to make that pivot. This chapter aims to assist with that decision-making process. First, however, I will share a reflection from my experience that led to the development of Integrated Library Planning.

Personal Narrative: Beginnings at Lancaster Theological Seminary Library

Within my first weeks as seminary librarian at Lancaster Theological Seminary in May 2014, it became quite clear that I had walked into the directorship of a library in the midst of many transitions. The first and most obvious transition was that of leadership. My predecessor had been director of the library for twenty-six years before he retired, and he spent the first year of his retirement continuing to work in the library part-time while the seminary conducted a search that eventually resulted in my arrival. The longer a person stays in a role the more the job responsibilities and institutional relationships to that role mold to fit that person's particular talents and preferences. Even if I had possessed nearly identical talents and preferences to my predecessor, it would have been difficult to step into a role that another person had held for a quarter of a century. As it is, I am quite different from my predecessor. Both the library and the seminary had to adjust to the absence of his talents that I did not possess and the arrival of new talents that I brought with me. I knew that my distinct working style and approach to library leadership would take months, if not years, to integrate into the seminary's culture.

In addition to leadership change, the library was also in the midst of an organizational transition. My predecessor carried the job title director of the library. Just a few short years before his retirement, before budget cuts made in the aftermath of the Great Recession, there were two professional librarians serving under his supervision in addition to a handful of paraprofessional assistants and student workers. At the time of my hire, I was to be the sole seminary librarian. The remainder of the staff consisted of one temporary full-time assistant who had been managing the day-to-day operation of the library for the past year, two part-time assistants, and a scant number of student workers. Seminary administrators expected that as temporary positions and retirements made way for newly created positions, I would fill these positions with paraprofessionals who would be paid salaries that could fit into the library's shrinking budget. Responsibilities that were once the focus of full-time professional librarians were either being managed *ad hoc* by paraprofessional assistants or had been set aside as low priority, awaiting future attention.

As my first few weeks stretched into my first few months at Lancaster Theological Seminary, I discovered that the library was embedded within an institution facing its own transitions. Walking into my first faculty meeting for the 2014–15 academic year, I quickly became acquainted with a topic that would reshape the seminary's educational mission: revising the curriculum to address the needs of bi-vocational students, meaning, students who would be attending school full time while working full time in one or more jobs. Any curriculum revision can send shockwaves into an academic library, but this curriculum revision had something more behind it. It was fueled by a realization that our students' contexts were changing, due in part to the changes underway in their communities and the vocations they would enter upon graduation. To remain effective and relevant as an educational institution, we needed to shift our curriculum to meet the new and different needs of our students resulting from the realities of their shifting contexts, communities, and vocational futures. The deeper I explored and researched my new position as librarian within this academic community, the more layers of transition I seemed to find. It was a time filled with change.

Accompanying these transitions were clear indicators of need impacting almost every aspect of library operation. The shelves were overcrowded in places and the administration gave me a mandate to significantly reduce the collection's size so that building space might be utilized differently. A significant portion of the seminary's archives were sitting in public areas of the library due to disorganization and overcrowding in the secure archives room. Boxes of sensitive records and documents were stacked on tables in reading areas and among the circulating book stacks. The integrated library system had barely changed since the library automated its catalog in 1996, with access to various staff modules restricted to individual computers. Off campus, students and faculty had access to a fraction of the library's electronic resources and only by referring URL technology through the seminary's student information system. The reduction of the library's staff had forced changes in the library's hours, which disgruntled many students. And while the library's acquisitions budget had been reduced consistently each year since the Great Recession, standing order commitments for continuing series had remained relatively the same, leaving little funds left for title selection in key subject areas that supported the seminary's curricula.

This was the state of the library when I began the journey toward Integrated Library Planning. The concept occurred to me as I was engaged in the interview process for the position. As a candidate for seminary librarian, I was given access to a report by a task force who had evaluated many aspects of the library and ultimately created the job description for a seminary librarian, departing from the library director model used for decades. This report gave me some insight into what changes the administration wanted to see and prompted me to ask several questions about how the task force had arrived at some of its conclusions. Who had been consulted? What future needs and trends are they anticipating and watching? Many of the recommendations in the task force report were reactions to what had been changing in the library since the Great Recession; I was also interested in anticipating future needs and dynamically responding to those in a forward-thinking way. I had been learning about Integrated Business Planning and began developing ideas to adapt it for a library context. By the time I was invited to interview on campus and present to the faculty, I had created a prototype of Integrated Library Planning which was the centerpiece of my vision for the library. After my hire and start as seminary librarian, I began trailblazing the path that would lead to our integrated plan and the Integrated Library Planning model.

Evaluating the Library's Pivot Potential

Before adopting a new planning model, it is crucial to evaluate the library's potential to pivot. Integrated Library Planning requires several kinds of shifts: a shift in approach to planning, a shift in style and frequency of assessment, and a shift in engagement with changes in and around the library. Such shifts suggest the concept of pivoting, a quick turning motion that takes as little room as possible. A pivot happens decisively. Once the Integrated Library Planning process begins, the library and its staff will be making a large pivot toward integration, followed by dozens of smaller pivots over time as the integrated plan develops and matures. Therefore, before beginning the process to create an integrated plan, it is wise to pause and consider the library's potential and tolerance for pivoting.

One helpful place to begin exploring the library's pivot potential is to look at the library's history of strategic planning. Is the library currently operating under a strategic plan? If so, how much time is left in the plan? If not, how long ago did the last strategic plan expire? What kind of energy surrounds strategic planning for the library? Does the library have planning processes that it finds effective and invigorating? Or does the library staff have little enthusiasm for strategic planning? What motivates the library staff to implement strategic plans? Are strategic plans implemented on a regular cycle because library staff find them helpful, or are they only implemented because they are deemed necessary or required by the library's parent organization or another external influence?

The answers to these questions will reveal a lot about the library's receptivity to Integrated Library Planning. For instance, a library that has been operating under strategic plans for some time, finds them effective, receives affirmation from its parent organization for implementing a strategic plan, and has a staff who is committed to the library's planning processes may not be interested in trying an integrated approach to planning. A library staff that is content with its planning practices may not see an incentive in changing and may prefer to continue using methods that have provided the library with good results in the past. Alternatively, a library that allowed its strategic plan to expire or implements a strategic plan for the sole purpose of satisfying a requirement imposed by a parent organization or other external influence and has a staff that feels rather lackluster about strategic planning might be interested in exploring Integrated Library Planning. A library with a staff that is frustrated by its existing or previous planning practices and is actively seeking a change would likely be open to making the necessary pivots for developing and implementing an integrated plan. A library with a staff that harbors a great deal of animosity or suspicion for any kind of planning process will likely need convincing and coaxing to try Integrated Library Planning and give it the commitment needed to succeed.

None of the hypothetical libraries described above are unsuitable for Integrated Library Planning. I would argue that any of them and their respective staff members would be a good candidate for trying an integrated plan. It is important to recognize, however, that some libraries may be more receptive than others to a change in approach to planning. Libraries that are primed for a new approach will likely be able to pivot toward Integrated Library Planning faster than libraries that are content with how they have always approached planning and libraries that are skeptical of any type of planning. If your library falls into one of the latter categories, then extra time and care may be needed to introduce Integrated Library Planning and build a case for it.

Another consideration in evaluating a library's potential to pivot toward Integrated Library Planning is its readiness for this new approach to planning. Readiness pertains to the current state of the library. As I mentioned in my personal narrative, the Lancaster Theological Seminary Library was in the midst of several transitions when I began pivoting it toward an integrated plan. Implementing an integrated planning process helped to bring some structure and order to the transitions that were already occurring in the library. The presence of transition is not necessary for a library's readiness. Other signs of readiness include positive energy for planning that is dynamic and responsive, curiosity for trying new things, and a restlessness with the status quo.

The presence of transition does not ensure a library's readiness, and some types of transitions may inhibit readiness for an integrated plan. As is the case with every human organization, libraries can carry a history of trauma. Libraries that are actively experiencing trauma or have recently experienced trauma will need time to heal before or in conjunction with pivoting toward an integrated plan. Certain types of crises and staffing transitions, especially those due to hostile or tragic circumstances, need time to resolve and settle before engaging the library staff in a new planning process. Some of the methods and practices described in the next chapter, such as hosting conversations, may help provide space for addressing, processing, and healing conflict and trauma that exists in the library. Paying attention to any trauma that exists in the library is critically important for determining readiness and must be factored into a pivot strategy for Integrated Library Planning.

One final consideration that is helpful when evaluating readiness for Integrated Library Planning is the matter of timing. If the library is currently operating under a strategic plan, when will that plan expire? Does the parent organization have a strategic plan and, if so, where is it in the strategic planning cycle? What are the annual rhythms of the library? When would it make sense to implement an integrated plan? What activities are going on in the library and its parent organization and what are the current commitments and responsibilities of the library staff that might impact the preparation work needed to set up an integrated plan?

Developing and implementing an integrated plan is an involved process that takes time, research, collaboration, and a lot of careful thought. While there is no ideal time to undertake the process, it is important to keep timeliness in mind so that the endeavor is not thwarted before it begins. Thankfully, Integrated Library Planning is designed to be flexible and organic, flowing with any change that occurs. Thus, as circumstances change during the early planning and development stages, the process can adapt to those changes. However, there are many recurring events and rhythms that it would be wise to account for: fiscal year cycles, vacation times, and holidays are a few. These rhythms may influence when a library might want to implement the monthly review cycle. Planning backward from that target implementation date will help determine a suitable timeframe for beginning the research and development process.

Building Support for Integrated Library Planning

Once a decision is made to begin an Integrated Library Planning process, it is important to make sure that all the library's stakeholder groups are on board with the decision and what comes with it. Since Integrated Library Planning is a slightly different approach to planning, with a rolling planning horizon and perpetual, inquiry-driven evaluation and assessment, library leaders will likely receive a variety of questions when the process begins. Taking time to introduce Integrated Library Planning helps to prepare everyone who will be involved in the planning process. The reactions and responses of key stakeholders are helpful and informative as the planning process and future workflows begin to take shape.

Before gathering support, it is essential to identify the library's stakeholder groups and their constituents. A stakeholder is anyone who has an interest in the library. It is helpful to group stakeholders according to a shared chief interest or other common factor. Stakeholder groups that are likely to be present in any library context are: library staff, administrators of the library's parent organization, donors, and patrons (subdivided by patron type). Individuals may likely belong to more than one stakeholder group. For example, a patron may also be a donor, and a library staff member may also be a patron. However, each individual stakeholder will identify with a primary group, determining how you interact with them when you introduce Integrated Library Planning.

Each stakeholder group has a different relationship to the library and a different set of interests in the library; therefore, introducing Integrated Library Planning looks different for each group. The purpose of this introduction is to raise awareness that the library is considering a new model for planning and to gain support. As will be described in later chapters, the process of developing an integrated plan is collaborative and consultative, engaging stakeholder groups at various times during the development process. Raising awareness and gathering support ahead of time helps to boost participation in the research and collaborative activities that inform the integrated plan, as well as support for the plan itself once it is implemented.

Those individuals who have some administrative role over the library director are the stakeholders who need to be communicated with first. In academic libraries, these are the deans, provosts, vice presidents, and presidents who provide oversight for the library and the library director. In other library contexts, this might be a library board, a board of trustees, or other individuals or a group that provides oversight and accountability for the library director. These stakeholders should already be receiving reports on the library's strategic plan and operations, and it is very important to make sure that they accept the shift to an integrated plan. Depending on the context and relationship between the library director and this stakeholder group, a formal proposal on Integrated Library Planning may or may not be needed. At the very least, it is important and wise to have a conversation with this group, or key members of this group, to outline the Integrated Library Planning process, highlight the outcomes, and present a draft timeline of the development process to implementation. The purpose at this point is to start a conversation and gain approval, if necessary, to continue moving forward. It is not necessary to have all the answers or to have every contingency planned out. What matters is making sure they are informed about the process and can lend their support moving forward.

Once the administrative stakeholders are on board, the next group to address are the library staff. Since this group is the most involved in every aspect of the plan's development and implementation, it is important to provide ample space and opportunity for library staff members to learn about Integrated Library Planning and ask questions. The library staff's commitment to engaging in the planning process is critical. Integrated Library Planning is very transparent, from development through implementation of the monthly review process. It is important to highlight this for staff as it may help to reduce anxiety and remove any mystery surrounding the plan. Anxiety may persist, however, as most changes and shifts in how things have been done previously produces some degree of anxiety among staff members. It is important to make space for this. Do not dismiss it out of hand. Acknowledge it. Make sure those staff members feel they are heard. Offer assurance as often and as best you can. Answering questions in a timely manner and providing as much detail as possible can sometimes help with reducing staff anxiety. At other times, the most assuring thing is a calm, confident, and supportive presence from the library leader.

A slightly different approach is needed when communicating with patrons and donors. The actual composition of these stakeholder groups will vary widely depending on a library's context. In an academic library context, patrons include faculty, non-library staff, students, alumni, and affiliate patrons (if the library is open to those outside the academic community). In a public library context, patron stakeholder groups might be grouped according to age (child, youth, adult, senior) or other clearly defined patron categories. Donors are loosely defined as stakeholders who support the library. This support may come in the form of financial support or volunteer support. If the library has a "friends" program, these individuals would be a stakeholder group. Otherwise, stakeholder groups might be defined by the type of support a donor provides the library.

Since these stakeholder groups are not involved in the day-to-day work of developing the integrated plan, communicating about Integrated Library Planning needs to take a slightly different tone. The objective is to alert these stakeholder groups that the library is about to engage in a new kind of planning process. The communication does not necessarily need to include specifics about the type of plan and a detailed timeline for development and implementation. Instead, focus on the positive outcomes that the library hopes for, and issue an invitation to participate. Assure these stakeholder groups that their input is valuable and important. Alert them that there will be several opportunities to participate in surveys and conversations about the library. It might also be helpful to provide a way for these stakeholders to express interest in becoming more involved. Compiling a list of interested stakeholders at this point will help tremendously with research later, for instance, streamlining the creation of focus groups. While these stakeholder groups do not need to give approval for the library's process, nor do they need to be committed to and engaged in it, keeping them informed and sharing the excitement of a new kind of planning is essential to the success of an integrated plan informed by the needs of the communities the library serves.

Assembling Teams and Tools

Before moving forward with an Integrated Library Planning process, it is helpful to gather the resources needed for the journey. Much like the concept of *mise en place* in cooking, gathering all the tools needed for planning and identifying who will be on the planning team prepares your physical and mental spaces for starting the planning process. This is not the time to start formal research for the plan, which is covered in the next chapter and is the first stage of the Integrated Library Planning process. Assembling teams and tools is about is making sure that you are prepared. Do you have all the information you need to embark on the adventure that is Integrated Library Planning? What additional resources and tools might be helpful? Who will be involved in the planning process? Do they have all the resources, tools, and training that they need for this to be a successful endeavor?

First, consider the question of your own readiness to develop an integrated plan. The first step might be to finish reading this book all the way through. While it is written to be a companion or guide through an Integrated Library Planning process, it is helpful to read it once entirely before actually starting the process. The same logic applies here as it does to reading a recipe all the way through before starting to cook or reviewing directions to go somewhere before starting to drive or walk to the destination. As you are reading, take note of concepts that are new or unfamiliar. Are there any concepts that warrant a closer look before starting to plan? Two resources in the back of the book, a list of additional resources in appendix A and the bibliography, can be used as a starting point for further reading on a wide range of topics and practices that may be incorporated into an Integrated Library Planning process. Going deeper into subjects like Gantt charts or mind maps, for example, might be extraordinarily helpful for librarians who have not used them much before. Learning more about these concepts in advance of using them decreases the amount of distraction that might arise and helps focus the work on the planning tasks at hand.

Since Integrated Library Planning is a model that can accommodate many methods and practices, consider if there are any methods or practices that would be helpful to add to your library's Integrated Library Planning process. What resources are needed for these additional methods, particularly to incorporate them into the plan and share them with the library staff participating in the planning process? Writing additional documentation or simple notes that outline how additional methods will be incorporated into the planning process is a valuable prework activity. These notes can be revisited when that stage of the plan is reached, acting as a custom appendix or companion to this book.

As you progress through this book, you will discover that Integrated Library Planning makes use of a variety of tools, including technologies and intentionally designed workflows. Each librarian, library leader, and planner has their own preferences when it comes to these types of tools. Regardless of whether you are a pen and paper planner or one who embraces computers and apps, it can be worthwhile to consider your tools for the library's planning process. Again, this is more about reducing future distractions by investigating options in advance. Any selections made at this point can always be changed later if a particular tool or workflow does not adequately fit the purpose. In fact, no decisions necessarily need to be made at this point. For example, if the library does not already use a project management application, researching and compiling notes on what is available and narrowing the choices down to two or three top considerations could be helpful. Thinking through these types of questions and anticipating what additional information might be helpful, before the planning process has begun, is a way of preparing for and imagining how an integrated plan might work for the library.

Finally, consider who will be part of the planning team. Chapter 5 describes the monthly review cycle in detail and offers several suggestions for the makeup of an Integrated Library Planning team that oversees this cycle, which becomes the driving force of the integrated plan once it is implemented. Understanding that there may be changes in staffing or in the design of the plan once planning has begun, it is worthwhile to consider who might be involved in monitoring and carrying out the monthly review cycle. These library staff members will be valuable companions, colleagues, and conversation partners during the Integrated Library Planning process. Do these staff members have the tools, resources, and training they need to be successful? As a follow-up to staff meetings when Integrated Library Planning is introduced, consider deeper conversations or training sessions with the librarians who will assist with the planning process. Unlike the stakeholder group conversations, the purpose of these meetings is to equip the staff for the work ahead. This will certainly be something to continue throughout the planning process, and testing a few key skills and concepts prior to beginning the planning period helps prepare everyone for what is coming and also helps acclimate the team to collaboration.

Summary

Starting an integrated plan is not something that can be done simply by reading this book and following its advice. It starts with a carefully considered decision. There are three steps that can help prepare the library for making that decision. Not necessarily a sequence, these steps are suggested to explore the library's capacity and aptitude for Integrated Library Planning. Taking time to explore this method of planning before beginning the planning process helps ensure the success of the plan and offers the opportunity to more fully develop skills that will be used. It is a chance to put a finger to the wind, dig deeper, test a few concepts in your library's context, and gauge whether this is a good fit.

The first step is to evaluate the library's potential to make the pivot to an integrated plan. At its core, Integrated Library Planning is dynamic and responsive and requires that the planners be as flexible as the plan. Some libraries and their communities are ready to embrace this. Others are not as ready. Evaluating the library's potential to pivot uncovers any factors that might hinder or slow a shift to an integrated plan. Hinderances might be a positive history with planning and little motivation to change, or it might be a traumatic history with planning or other tragic event that needs to be resolved before moving forward with a new planning process. This is also the time to look at the calendar and rhythms of the library, its parent organization, and the surrounding community. Pivoting to an integrated plan must be well-timed: when the season is right, and the key people involved in planning are ready.

The second step is to build support for Integrated Library Planning. This involves identifying all the library's stakeholder groups and their constituent stakeholders, as well as sharing appropriately about starting an Integrated Library Planning process. Integrated Library Planning is designed as a very transparent process with free-flowing communication between all departments within the library, library administration, and the administrative personnel or body that oversees the library director. It is important to start with transparency when engaged in the process of deciding whether to proceed with an integrated plan.

Approaching individuals who have an administrative role over the library director about Integrated Library Planning engages them in the library's exploratory process, opens conversation about what a plan needs to provide or accomplish, and creates opportunity for approval or affirmation to move forward. When introducing Integrated Library Planning to library staff, the main objective is to give staff members a voice in the decision, a chance to ask questions, and encouragement to engage in a new approach to planning and assessment. It is also helpful to communicate with stakeholder groups that include patrons and donors, even though they are not employees of the library. Sharing that the library may soon be starting something new is a way to generate interest and excitement in supporting the library through the transition to the new plan. Stakeholder participation in surveys, feedback forms, and focus groups enhances the background research that informs the integrated plan. Inviting this feedback early in the process may help increase response rates once development of the plan is underway.

The third step is to assemble the teams and tools that are needed for an Integrated Library Planning process. Gathering all the resources before the planning process begins helps to prepare everyone more fully for the work ahead. This step also includes becoming familiar with all the stages and components of Integrated Library Planning, considering how the outline presented in this book might be customized to fit your library's context, reviewing and preselecting tools and workflows that may be helpful, and identifying the people who will be part of the core planning team. Some additional reading or research might be helpful. Additional training in a few skills or applications might be necessary to ensure a smooth and successful planning process. This step is your opportunity to make sure the spaces are prepared and all teams are adequately equipped to begin this new method of planning.

Once the timing of a pivot is determined, the necessary people have been consulted, and all is prepared, a decision to move forward with an integrated plan can be made. The chapters ahead explore the four stages of developing and implementing an integrated plan. It is an exciting time but take care to balance eagerness with attentiveness. Walk carefully through each stage of the planning process. Ask many questions. Observe closely. Analyze and synthesize all the findings. Write in pencil, and do not be afraid to return to a previous place for a second look or attempt. Are you ready?

Preliminary: Pivoting toward an integrated future
Stage 1: Foundation and groundwork
Stage 2. Building a planning structure
Stage 3. Implementing a monthly review cycle
Stage 4. Long-term assessment and adjustment

CHAPTER 3

Foundation and Groundwork

Every organization or relationship relies on a strong foundation from which it can grow and flourish. Integrated Library Planning is no different. The foundation and groundwork that happens at the start of a library's integrated plan is incredibly important. This initial stage supports all the planning work that follows. It is not a place to take shortcuts or to make assumptions. Nine months is a good length of time for this stage, but I recommend taking no less than six months and probably no more than twelve months.

During the first stage of Integrated Library Planning, you will engage in four areas of research about your library: gathering background information; developing mission and vision statements; assessing needs; and compiling strengths, weakness, opportunities, and threats. It is not a true linear process and works best if these avenues of research are pursued organically and concurrently. Start with the first one and work as far as you can until you feel ready to move to the next. As you engage the research process, be aware of gaps in your knowledge and understanding. Are there additional questions to ask or conclusions that need to be revisited? Are there emerging themes that need to be explored further in the context of your previous research? This back-and-forth organic mode of inquiry will help you to collect and analyze a wide variety of data in this stage, creating a strong foundation for the development of the library's integrated plan.

Gathering Background Information

As you begin the planning process, it is important to gather as much information about your library and its parent institution as you can. If you have been at your library for a while, it might be helpful to adopt the mindset of someone meeting your library for the first time. Gather a broad range of facts and data that will give you as complete a picture as possible of the library. When a person prepares for a job interview, she researches the background of the organization with whom she is interviewing. A similar mode of inquiry goes into gathering background information for Integrated Library Planning.

The library, like any organization, exists within three types of environments. These environments can be illustrated as concentric circles, like layers of an onion (see figure 1). The innermost circle is the intimate environment. This is the culture of the library itself: the staff makeup, departmental organization, the

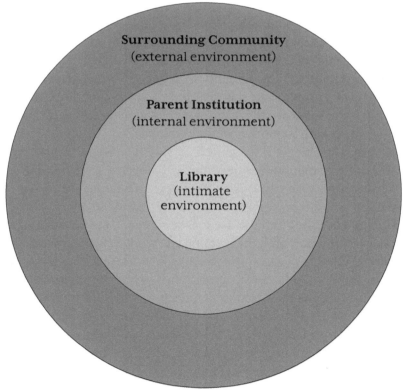

FIGURE 1
A library's three environments.

collection size and foci. Just beyond the intimate environment is the internal environment. This is the culture of the institution or organization that the library functions within. For an academic library, the internal environment is the parent educational institution or consortium of educational institutions. For a public library, the internal environment might be the municipal government that supports the library's budget and programs or a regional library consortium. Beyond the internal environment is the external environment. While the external environment could include everything else beyond the internal environment to a national or global scale, it is helpful to limit the external environment to those external forces that have an immediate impact on the library. This is usually confined to the community found within a geographically defined area around your library, or it might include communities your library serves through partnerships with other libraries.

While gathering background information, it is important to attend to each of these environments. Documents and resources that you find may only address the intimate or internal environments. Every library, regardless of type, can benefit from attending to its external environment. Patrons enter the library from the external environment, carrying with them a set of needs and expectations that librarians may be oblivious to if they are only attentive to the intimate and internal environments. Likewise, inward reflection on the library's own culture is vitally important. The way in which the library is organized and how it functions has a deep impact on the way in which it carries out its services.

Gathering background information does not have to be a daunting research project. It is likely that documents providing background information from each of the three environments already exist. Once you identify and compile these documents, additional research may be conducted to fill gaps. The types of documents needed and available will vary greatly depending on the type of library and its planning history. In general, there are two types of background documents to look for: institutional histories and previous planning documents.

Mining Institutional History

Institutional histories are extremely helpful in that they reveal how the library has developed over time and how the community and user populations have changed. Sometimes an institutional history or historical document exists independent of any other document. For example, a college or university may have its history recorded in a published volume. Many municipalities also have histories that could include information about the establishment and development of

30   Chapter 3

the public library. Published histories are not the only source of institutional memory, however. The library's collection development policy may contain a section on the history of the library and its collections. Other sources of institutional history include older promotional materials, committee and task force reports, and reports compiled for accreditation (in the case of academic libraries) or other outside assessment and review. If the library is a department within a larger organization, it may be helpful to consult with other administrators within the organization to identify and locate relevant documents.

Previous Planning Documents

If your library has ever engaged in a planning process, past planning documents may be revisited and revised for the integrated plan. When using previous planning documents, it is crucial to think of them as artifacts and resources, not necessarily as a starting point for the new integrated plan. The caution here is not to use past information gathering as a shortcut in the current planning process. If you were not involved in the previous planning process, you cannot know for certain how thoroughly the background research was conducted. Even if the previous plan was created in the not-so-distant past and you were involved in or led the process, it is important to view the background information contained in the previous plan with a critical eye.

Case Study

The library at Ovington Community College explored starting an integrated plan and, having decided on moving forward, is gathering background information. The first task for the library director is to identify the library's environments so that they can begin researching the background of each. The intimate environment is the library itself, which comprises a 15-member staff. The internal environment is Ovington Community College, which has one campus plus an online learning environment. The external environment is the city and county where the community college is located because this is where most of the students and alumni reside.

The library has had previous strategic plans, and the library director starts with these to begin collecting information about the library's history and context. The library's collection development policy also includes a background statement that the library director gathers with the information from previous strategic plans. Since the library exists within Ovington Community College, information about the school's history and background are also important to study. The library director finds a lot of useful background information in the school's current strategic plan. To round out the picture of the community college, the library director also researches reports made by the president to the school's trustees, as well as admissions reports from the past few years. A brief look into the local history helps ground the school in its geographical location and context, and the library director finds many insights in demographic research on the municipalities that utilize the community college. This research includes US Census data and statistics from school districts that feed into the community college.

The process of researching this background information is completed by generating a written narrative. Writing up his findings, the library director discovers many correlations between the surrounding community and the mission and vision of the community college. Several questions also emerge as the picture comes together of how the library fits within the community college and the geographic area surrounding it. In some cases, the library director searches for and finds answers in additional institutional documents. Those questions that remain unanswered are recorded in a separate document to be reviewed after more foundation and groundwork for the integrated plan is underway.

Mission and Vision Statements

When enough background information has been gathered to create a somewhat comprehensive picture of the library, it is time to move on to developing mission and vision statements. Many books and articles have been written about the process of composing mission and vision statements. My purpose is not to rehash what has already been written on the subject but instead to place mission and vision statements within the context of the Integrated Library Planning process.

The mission statement in an integrated plan states the library's purpose, its reason for being. In many ways, it is the essence of what the library does. The vision statement in an integrated plan states the library's aspiration, what it hopes to become or achieve. It fills in the blank: "When functioning at its best, this library…" The two statements are related to one another: mission and vision are complementary, not competing nor duplicating. The mission statement is usually shorter and pithier. It is something that might appear prominently on the library's website or in a brochure and could be adapted for a tagline or catchphrase. The vision statement is usually longer, with more detail and nuance. It may be patterned similarly to the mission statement but must go beyond simply expanding upon it. The vision needs to be a deeper statement of how the library envisions itself when it is fully living into its mission.

Developing mission and vision statements is a multistep process. It involves the initial crafting of the statements, followed by a process of vetting the statements with key stakeholder groups. Both steps can be taken prior to moving on to needs assessment, and they will likely be revisited at multiple points. The mission and vision statements will likely not be finalized until the very end of this initial stage of foundation and groundwork.

Crafting Statements

Many years have passed since mission and vision statements first gained popularity among organizations, so it is likely that your library has an existing mission statement to use as a starting point. Even if your library does not have an existing mission or vision statement, the larger parent organization likely does. These existing mission statements can be helpful in crafting a new mission statement for the integrated plan. They should not, however, restrict the library from exploring its mission and vision thoroughly.

There are several different methods and practices for crafting mission and vision statements. In situations where a chief librarian has a small or nonexistent staff, crafting the first draft statements may be a solitary endeavor. Larger libraries will likely want to charge a committee with engaging in a collaborative process. Regardless, the initial drafts of the statements are simply that: drafts. Save any notes from discussions or rumination that led to the first draft of the statements. These notes may be helpful later when revising the statements before they are finalized.

Vetting Statements

Once the mission and vision statements have been drafted, the more important work of vetting the statements with key stakeholders begins. To get the maximum amount of feedback about the drafted statements, engage stakeholders in personal one-on-one or small group conversations. Have the statements printed or displayed for stakeholders to read and ponder before offering their feedback. While email and social media can be a helpful mode of conversation and feedback for some things, developing mission and vision statements carry a weight and importance that demand a deeper level of engagement and discussion. In personal conversations about mission and vision statements, observing a stakeholder's body language, inflection, and energy level is as important as recording their feedback and suggestions.

After the first drafts of mission and vision statements are vetted, the process will likely lead to creative revision. Revision should be followed with more vetting, involving the same or perhaps different stakeholders. When the mission and vision statements have been sufficiently vetted and are ready to be tested, it is time to move on to needs assessment. It is important to remember that what comes out of needs assessment may impact the mission and vision statements. Be prepared to revisit this process if needed.

Case Study

Woodson Library serves a small liberal arts college. The head librarian is assisted by four other professional librarians and a cadre of student workers. The library already has a mission statement that has been in use for five years. As the library's five-year strategic plan draws to a close, the head librarian seeks to open conversation about the library's mission statement in preparation for a transition to an integrated plan. The head librarian starts by meeting with the four professional librarians on staff to ask their opinions on the current mission statement. The conversation reveals that the mission statement no longer fits the library. There is room for adjustment so that a revised mission statement may reflect the library's current, forward-looking position within the college.

Using the current mission statement as a starting point, the head librarian begins listing notable qualities of the library that have emerged during their information gathering about the library, college, and the broader community. The head librarian tries grouping them into categories and looks for a common theme or set of themes. Comparing this list with the current mission statement, they see where the language could be updated, modernized, and tailored for the library's current strengths.

Woodson Library does not already have a vision statement, so developing a vision statement will be a new endeavor for the library. The college does have a set of statements that include mission, vision, and values. The head librarian lists those next to the library's current mission statement and the compiled list of notable qualities. Viewing these statements and terms side by side allows the head librarian to draft new mission and vision statements that draw on all these resources, establishing a distinct yet connected mission and vision for the library.

Once new mission and vision statements are drafted, the head librarian begins seeking feedback on them. First, the four professional librarians on staff who gave feedback on the current mission statement review the newly drafted mission and vision statements. Next, the head librarian shares the statements with the library's student workers, asking for their perspectives as both library staff and college students. Finally, they share the statements with a few faculty members who are avid library users and strong advocates. All the feedback the head librarian receives is helpful and instructive, informing several adjustments to wording. The draft statements are stronger than when they started and are more robust and forward-thinking than the library's current mission statement. The drafts are sufficient to move on to the next stage of information gathering.

Needs Assessment

With clear knowledge and understanding of institutional history, current location and environments, and equipped with mission and vision statements to test, it is time to engage in a full needs assessment. This is the most time intensive component of the foundation and groundwork stage. This is where much of the discovery and learning about the library and its users happens. Oftentimes, new knowledge emerges, impacting the mission and vision statements. This is where the organic nature of the process comes to bear. As information is collected and evaluated during the needs assessment, be prepared to revisit the mission and vision statements or go back to background research, if necessary. This is not a process to rush. Rather, it is an opportunity to observe and ponder.

Needs assessment involves evaluating the needs of both the library and its community of users. Regarding the library, examine the building, spaces, infrastructure, systems, and equipment. What works well? What is not working well? Is anything outdated or in disrepair? Look at the collections and holdings as well. How are they growing or changing? How much is being invested in developing the collections? Then shift to examining usage. How is the library being used, by whom, and when? What questions are users asking most often? What are the most and least checked out items? Are there any unanswered questions or requests that go unfulfilled by the library? The goal of this line of questioning is to create a comprehensive profile of both the library and its user community.

This is one of many areas within Integrated Library Planning that may accommodate a wide range of methodologies. There are many methods that can be combined and utilized for a needs assessment. When selecting methods, however, it is important to employ a variety of data types and engage all stakeholder groups. This means collecting both quantitative and qualitative data on your users and your library. It involves looking at statistics and numbers as well as leaving the desk to observe what is happening in the library. Conversations with stakeholders, both formal and informal, are crucial to understanding the dynamics between the library and its users. Engaging multiple methods for data collection and analysis will provides a more robust picture for needs assessment. In the following sections I describe the four methods that were most helpful for needs assessment at my library. Feel free to add to or adapt these to fit your library and context.

Statistics and Usage Patterns

Most librarians are familiar with gathering statistics on library usage to share with administrative bodies and funding agencies. This is an opportunity to examine these statistics to determine what they are saying about the library and its users. Comparing statistical data from year to year can be helpful in identifying and projecting trends.

Start by gathering the statistics and reports compiled in the past. It may be helpful to go back three to five years. Organize the statistics and reports into groups by type. Helpful areas to look at are budget reports, collection development, circulation, website traffic, electronic resources, visitors, program attendance, reference inquiries, and patron enrollment. Once the statistics and reports are gathered, look to see what might be missing. In some cases, it may be possible to run a few new reports from the integrated library system to fill the gaps. In other cases, especially counting visitors and program attendance, it may not be possible to gather this kind of historical data.

Analyzing the gathered data can be done in multiple ways. Tables of numbers are often the easiest method, giving the clearest information when precise comparisons are needed. For visual learners, however, converting tables of numbers into charts and graphs can help immensely. A line graph of circulation statistics, for example, can amplify usage trends and rhythms. Noticing an increase in circulation at certain times of the year might prompt research into the most used items during those times of the year. If similar patterns repeat every year, a clear need exists for these items at specific times of the year.

Experienced librarians may intuit many of these needs. However, it is helpful and important to check intuition with quantitative data. Taking a close look at a variety of statistics across the library side by side may reveal connections that are subtle and less intuitive. The purpose is to uncover and discover needs of both the library and its users, even if these statistics were originally collected and used for a different purpose. Library statistics are often reported for metrics, a measure

36   Chapter 3

of the library's performance and the collection's strength. Whatever conclusions were reached when analyzing this data for reporting metrics may need to be suspended temporarily to make space for a new analysis concerning needs.

Equally important as reviewing historical data from past statistical reports is collecting real-time data on current usage patterns. This can be done by making a series of observations about the library and its users in a structured and focused way during an appropriate period. Observations and data collected will depend upon the type of library and specifics of the library's context. A few basic, guiding questions to use as a starting point are: How many people are in the library at given points during the day? What types of activities are they engaged in? Are there certain places in the library that draw more people than others? What types of materials and resources are being used in house, and are there any correlations between in-house use and what is checked out?

Collect some questions like this and draw up a research and observation plan. Consider and decide on types of behavior to observe, and map these to the questions. Keep in mind that some observations may help to answer multiple questions. Create a schedule for when these observations will be collected and a plan for how to collect them. Enlist the library staff to assist and collect observations at various points during the day on a schedule over a few weeks. At the end of the period, assemble the data into tables and charts to be considered with everything else that's being collected during the needs assessment.

Formal Surveys and Patron Feedback

Taking a deeper look at your statistics and collecting observations of usage patterns are indirect ways of discovering the needs of patrons. Administering formal surveys and soliciting feedback from patrons are direct approaches and equally as important. Combining direct feedback with indirect observations and data gathering can offer a more holistic picture of both library and user needs.

There are several different methods for surveying patrons and stakeholders. The methods chosen should match various stakeholders' preferences. For example, a library serving a diverse community with multiple generations may need one type of survey instrument designed for children and youth and a second survey instrument designed for adults. Libraries with user populations not adept with online surveys may choose to administer a printed or telephone survey.

There are several resources available for writing and administering effective surveys. While this book does not review the breadth and depth of these resources, here are a few basic tips to start. Great care must be taken to craft questions that invite thoughtfulness, honesty, and completion. Surveys that are too long or require too many open-ended responses may result in abandoned surveys or incomplete results. Return rates for surveys are also known for being low, so incentives may be necessary to encourage participation. A drawing for gift cards, free books, or library swag might be helpful to motivate stakeholders to participate in surveys.

Another way to encourage patrons and stakeholders to share their thoughts about the library is by providing multiple pathways for feedback. Does your library have a suggestion box or place to leave comments? If so, then some promotion or attention to the means to leave feedback may be enough to prompt participation. Social media may also be helpful in soliciting feedback but requires an active user base to be effective. In the absence of an existing suggestion box or active social media following, try creating a temporary comment box and placing it at the circulation desk or another place where patrons spend time and are likely to notice it. Offer a simple, open prompt that invites a patron or other stakeholder to jot a quick response and drop it in the box. Be creative with the prompt. The key is to get the patron's attention and make it easy for them to respond quickly and thoughtfully in that moment. If patrons are not able to respond completely in that moment, they are not likely to return to complete the feedback later.

Survey responses and feedback forms can be processed and analyzed similarly to statistical data. Most electronic survey applications offer basic analytical tools that convert responses into easy-to-read charts and graphs. Even surveys that are collected in a print form could be re-entered into the electronic survey application for inclusion in the analysis. Open-ended responses can be organized and categorized with values assigned for easier analysis. Quantitative data collected through statistics, observations, surveys, and feedback forms is incredibly helpful for beginning to identify and assess the needs of a library and its users.

Hosting Conversations

For a more nuanced understanding of the library and its users, it is also necessary to gather qualitative data. While surveys and feedback forms often include open-ended questions, data collected is commonly filtered through a print or electronic, text-based medium. Qualitative data can also be collected through direct human interaction, spoken and visual. These types of interactions have added layers that can shed additional light on needs assessment. Oftentimes the librarian approaches qualitative data gathering with a specific question and hypothesis that will be tested as they collect responses. While this is an acceptable way to collect and incorporate qualitative data into the needs assessment, I would like to present an alternative approach: hosting conversations.

The practice of hosting conversations is promoted by a self-organized international community called the Art of Hosting. I first learned about this community from *Walk Out Walk On* by Deborah Frieze and Margaret Wheatley. The Art of Hosting user community collects and shares conversational practices and wisdom about using them to facilitate change in a community or organization. The core concept is that transformation can happen when leaders are good hosts instead of trying to play the role of hero or heroine, something that particularly resonated with me. Being a good host involves invitation, creating a welcoming space, and attending to the environment and participants in a way that leads to fruitful conversation. It is a way of facilitating conversations that are open to exchanging ideas and building relationships.

There are many practices used by the Art of Hosting user community. Circle, World Café, and Open Space Technology are just a few. Incorporating Art of Hosting practices into the needs assessment process can have a powerful and profound effect on the integrated plan. For example, a small academic library with low alumni engagement invites alumni to participate in a circle conversation. Special, personal invitations are sent out to individuals identified as potential participants. A simple space is prepared in the library to host the conversation: an intimate space with a circle of chairs. In the center of the circle is a focal piece that represents the library or the season, perhaps books with a floral arrangement or school spirit items. Two library staff members convene the circle and lead the participants through a few open-ended prompts: What brings you to the circle today? Share a recent experience when you needed help finding answers or solving a problem and its outcome. Considering these shared experiences, how might the library better assist alumni in those moments? What new thoughts or ideas do you carry away from the circle?

On the surface, the questions are not much different from open-ended essay questions that might be included on a survey form. If asked these questions in a written survey, or even in a one-on-one interview situation, the respondent would only be able to speak to their own experience. When asked within a circle conversation, the respondents bring their individual experiences together to form a collective. The circle creates a unique dynamic that allows patterns and themes to emerge more quickly and facilitates more creativity and exchange of ideas as the participants become informed by each other's experiences.

Circle is just one example of many styles of conversation practices that can be hosted within a library for needs assessment. The style or type of conversation a library may host will depend upon the stakeholders and the type of wisdom or sharing that would be most helpful for the needs assessment. The principles of hosting—creating space, invitation, and openness—remain the same regardless of conversation practice.

Hosting conversations can be particularly meaningful and valuable for libraries that have experienced some tension or conflict in the past. If patrons have been particularly unhappy with a library service or a change in hours, hosting a conversation is a way to bring all concerned parties together and attempt to heal the damaged relationships. Everyone has a voice in a hosted conversation, and the librarian's job as facilitator is to listen more than to speak. The group can spend a few minutes at the beginning to agree upon a set of rules to guide the conversation in a respectful and helpful manner. The ensuing conversation allows everyone a chance to make their voice heard, to collaborate on solutions that address the concerns, and to rebuild more positive relationships between library and stakeholders.

Hosting conversations can transform the way you understand your library and its users. There are numerous resources available on Art of Hosting and the various conversation practices it incorporates, many of which are listed in appendix A. Facilitator and practitioner trainings are also incredibly helpful. One does not necessarily need to attend a training to be able to host a conversation, however. All that is needed is a little preparation and an open mind.

Appreciative Inquiry

Drawing from the Art of Hosting philosophy, I have found the practice of Appreciative Inquiry to be particularly helpful in Integrated Library Planning. This conversational practice was originally developed by David Cooperrider at Case Western Reserve University. In its pure form, Appreciative Inquiry is a four-part cycle consisting of discovery, dream, design, and destiny. For many organizations, all stakeholders participate in each part of the cycle. For a library, however, the types of stakeholders vary more than within another type of organization. For that reason, I adapt Appreciative Inquiry to maximize its effectiveness across the range of stakeholders, from staff to patrons (see figure 2).

The starting point for Appreciative Inquiry is a positive core question. Composing a good, powerful question is an art, and it may take multiple tries to settle on the one that will work the best. The chief library administrator

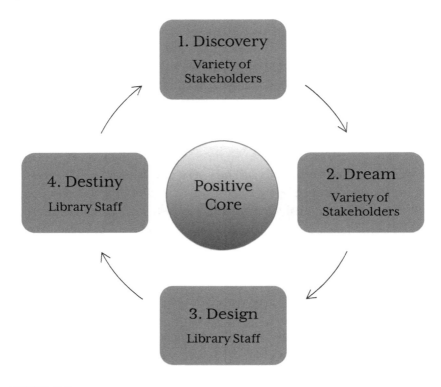

FIGURE 2
An adaptation of the Appreciative Inquiry 4-D cycle for use by libraries and librarians as part of an integrated plan, based on a similar chart from *The Power of Appreciative Inquiry* by Diana Whitney and Amanda Trosten-Bloom.

and a small group of trusted library staff are usually tasked with generating the powerful question. It should be open, yet not too broad. It should provoke thought, spark imagination, and invite conversation. The powerful question fuels the positive core of Appreciative Inquiry; therefore, it needs to avoid evoking negative emotions or memories. The purpose is not to cover up or gloss over any pain or harm of the past or present. Rather, it is intended to help participants acknowledge it and move forward with a focus on repair and positive change.

Once the positive core is established with a powerful question, the four-part cycle may begin. The first two steps—discovery and dream—take place in conversation with as many stakeholder groups as possible. Using the principles of the Art of Hosting, this may take place as hosted conversations facilitated by library staff in the library or other appropriate, welcoming place. There are many ways to host this conversation and make sure that all are represented and have a voice. Depending on the library's context, one option is to host a single conversation with representatives from each stakeholder group. Another option might be to host multiple conversations, each with a different stakeholder group or different combinations of stakeholders. The goal is to involve as many people as possible in the conversation.

The conversation has two parts, one for each of the first two parts of the Appreciative Inquiry cycle. The first is "discovery," when participants consider "What gives life?" This is about appreciating and recognizing the best of what is. To get to this part, the facilitator frames the powerful question in a way that prompts reflection on the positive aspects of the library, its collections, and its services in the present moment. For example, if the powerful question is "How can the library be the community's hub?" then discovery would involve calling forth all the ways in which the library engages the community at present.

The second part of the conversation shifts into the "dream" phase, when participants consider "What could be?" This is about imagining opportunities for the future. The facilitator collects notes and observations from the discovery round and presents them back to the group. This is a time to make connections and draw out themes. The themes usually indicate aspects of the library that resonate with stakeholders. These are positive aspects that could be further developed in the dream phase. In our example, participants might share in the discovery phase how the library hosts community events and offers access to resources specific to the community. In the dream phase, the questions and conversation shift to how these services could be enhanced so that the library becomes a true hub for the community. A brainstorming session follows in which participants imagine community events on a variety of topics and share ideas for displaying and promoting resources.

These conversations with stakeholders do not need to be marathon events. An hour is usually sufficient to make introductions, pose the question for discovery, collect observations to identify themes, pose the question for dreaming, collect ideas, and then close. Larger groups may take more than an hour to allow time for everyone to speak. One way to facilitate a larger group is to allow participants to discuss the discovery question in pairs for a few minutes and then share a summary of their conversation with the group. It is usually helpful to have participants sit in a circle so that everyone may see each other. The facilitator may want a board to post the questions and record observations, themes, and ideas. It also may be helpful to have a co-facilitator who can take notes while the other facilitates the conversation.

42   Chapter 3

Once the conversations with stakeholders are held, the first two steps of the Appreciative Inquiry cycle are complete. At this point, the chief library administrator convenes the library staff for the third and fourth steps of the cycle. The third step is "design," when participants ask "What should be?" The fourth step is "destiny," when participants collectively discern "What will we do?" Notes from the discovery and dream conversations with stakeholders inform these library staff conversations. Any other research and data collected up to this point in the foundation and groundwork stage may also be shared and considered. The objective is for the library staff to build on the brainstorms from all stakeholders within the realm of possibility. Design is the conversational process of building upon the dreams of stakeholders to create a vision that is achievable.

Once a vision is built, the chief library administrator leads the staff through the process in determining the next action steps. When used within Integrated Library Planning, the destiny step is expanded into the next stages of the integrated plan. At this point, in the foundation and groundwork stage, Appreciative Inquiry enables the staff to envision the positive change that is desired from the integrated plan and have the beginnings of a framework to use in the next stage to begin to enact that vision.

The process of leading staff through the design and destiny steps of Appreciative Inquiry can be tailored to the library's context. In some cases, a day-long retreat setting might be the most efficient way to work through these steps, breaking the discussion time up between the large group and smaller working groups. However, day-long retreats are not always appropriate or possible for all library staffs. Alternatives include a series of staff meetings to work through clusters of topics or individual working group meetings preceding a longer staff meeting. There is not one correct way to engage in this process. Rather, feel encouraged to experiment and thoughtfully reflect on what might work best in your context.

Case Study

The Parks Community Library is preparing a needs assessment for its integrated plan. The current library director has only been in the position for one year and relies on the reports and records from the previous library director to begin compiling data about usage patterns. As part of the library's annual reporting to the municipality, the library director has access to several years of statistics on circulation, acquisitions, purchase suggestions, and interlibrary loan. The outreach librarian has kept thorough records of all the programs the library has held over the past three years, including the attendance recorded on the day of each event. The reference librarians have some statistics for reference questions they have received, but they have not kept a complete count.

The library director pulls together these statistics and begins examining them. Several possible trends begin to emerge. Three fiction genres dominate purchase suggestions while a few nonfiction subject areas are the most requested from interlibrary loan. Cross-referencing interlibrary loan requests with the reference desk log suggests that at least half of interlibrary loan requests are a direct result of a patron's interview with a reference librarian. Daily circulation totals show small spikes on the same day programs were held, though there are also high rates of circulation on days and during weeks when few programs were offered.

Based on these observations from the library's statistics and usage data, the library director develops a few different survey tools. One is an electronic survey about reference services, sent to all known patrons who contacted the reference desk within the last year. Another electronic survey is about purchase suggestions, sent to all patrons who made a purchase suggestion within the last year. One of the questions on the purchase suggestion survey is about interlibrary loan since there seems to be a difference between purchase suggestions and requests from interlibrary loan. The library director also asks the outreach librarian to begin circulating feedback forms at programs and sets out a comment box at the circulation desk with a simple form asking "How did we do today?"

After three months of collecting these surveys and feedback forms, the library director examines the new information alongside the data originally gathered. While the response rate was only a fraction of the patrons who used the library during this time period, there are enough responses to gain a more detailed picture of the library and its patrons. Tying in these new insights with the background information gathered earlier, the library director starts working on a powerful question that can be used for Appreciative Inquiry conversations with focus groups comprised of representative stakeholders. In a library staff meeting, the director presents a summary of what has been learned through the surveys and feedback along with a draft of the powerful question. The staff spends forty-five minutes discussing the data, brainstorming on the powerful question, and considering how to invite stakeholders to join the focus groups. By the end of the staff meeting, the library director has a powerful question finalized and clear direction for focus group invitations.

The patrons who answered the surveys and indicated a willingness to participate in a focus group belong mostly to one category of stakeholders: engaged patrons and members of the community. The library director taps into the fundraising records to identify major donors to the library and sends invitations to join a focus group. The library director also reaches out to the elected officials and municipal overseers who evaluate the library on an annual basis. To round out the focus groups, the library director works with the youth librarian to adapt the powerful question and Appreciative Inquiry model for a focus group of children and another focus group of teens.

The library holds the focus group conversations with these stakeholder groups over the course of a month. Using the Appreciative Inquiry model, the librarians facilitating the conversations lead the participants through sets of questions designed to prompt discovering and appreciating what works well at the library, then dreaming and imagining what the library could be doing in the future. The facilitators take copious notes during these sessions and give these to the library director, who then collects them and creates a summary document for the next library staff meeting. After reviewing all the comments and information collected during the focus group conversations, the library staff begin the work of designing and innovating what changes the library might implement. The ideas generated in the staff meeting are recorded, and the library director takes them forward into the next stages of the integrated planning process.

By combining multiple types of data and a variety of methods for collecting feedback and comments from patrons and other stakeholders, the Parks Community Library now has a much more intricate and detailed picture of how it is serving the community and a much richer collection of ideas for carrying the library into the future. Without the focus groups, for example, the library director might have made mistaken assumptions about what changes or innovations patrons would want. Taking the time to ask additional questions that emerged from looking at data collected as part of the library's daily work helped the library staff better understand what is most relevant to patrons. All of this will feed directly into an integrated plan that will be timely and relevant for the library's staff members and patrons.

Strengths, Weaknesses, Opportunities, and Threats

At this point, the foundation and groundwork stage has involved collecting and analyzing data, conducting research, and getting to know the library and its stakeholders on a variety of levels. A drafted mission and vision statement has likely been revisited and revised as the needs assessment process continued. Once this work is nearing completion, you are ready to evaluate strengths, weaknesses, opportunities, and threats—SWOTs for short.

Creating a SWOT matrix can help bring the focus back out to the big picture reality of the library. At each point in foundation and groundwork, focus has shifted from one area to another. A SWOT matrix brings all the information from each environment, each stakeholder group, and each idea or area of vision and collates it into a single table. It is a powerful tool that presents a comprehensive view of the library with all its assets and challenges. The exercise of creating a SWOT matrix helps to synthesize all that is learned throughout the foundation and groundwork stage. The finished table serves as an excellent reference for internal use and for sharing with administrative overseers.

A SWOT matrix has four quadrants determined by the combination of two factors. Qualities of the library are placed in the quadrants according to the factors that created them. Along the horizontal axis is the type of impact, positive or negative. Along the vertical axis is origin, internal or external. When the horizontal and vertical intersect, a matrix is created with four quadrants (see figure 3). Strengths are placed in the upper left quadrant, where positive or

FIGURE 3
A SWOT matrix.

46   Chapter 3

helpful qualities originate internally. Weaknesses are placed in the upper right quadrant, where negative or harmful qualities originate internally. Opportunities are placed in the lower left quadrant, where positive or helpful qualities originate externally. Threats are placed in the lower right quadrant, where negative or harmful qualities originate externally.

There are several different ways to fill a SWOT matrix. One is to list all the factors of the library that have been discovered so far and start matching them to the appropriate quadrant. Another is to reflect on each quadrant individually as it relates to the research conducted and information gathered. The chief library administrator could generate the SWOT matrix alone, or it could be a task undertaken by committee. It is helpful to keep it to one page; therefore, the information placed in the matrix needs to be succinct. Do not use overly complicated or complex abbreviations to save space. This will only make it more difficult to read later. Keep the language short, simple, and direct. Remember that the details exist in all the statistical reports and documents collected throughout this stage. The SWOT matrix serves to summarize all those reports in a tool where they can be easily evaluated.

Once a library's assets and challenges are recorded in a SWOT matrix, the information in the matrix can be leveraged as the integrated plan begins to form. Strengths uncovered during the review of statistical data can now be viewed alongside weaknesses revealed by background documents. Opportunities discovered during an Appreciative Inquiry conversation are now in direct conversation with threats unveiled by environmental scans.

Hopefully, the SWOT matrix will be balanced with an equal number of qualities listed in each quadrant. If any one side is out of balance, it might indicate that additional research is needed. If the matrix is top-heavy with more qualities recognized for internal origin, then additional research is needed on the library's external environment. If the matrix is right-heavy with more negative or harmful challenges, then additional conversations with stakeholders may help to uncover more positive assets. The matrix does not need to be perfectly balanced; however, the weight of each quadrant should be close to the others.

Case Study

The Du Bois Library is nearing the end of its information gathering stage for creating an integrated plan. The library director begins to summarize the findings in a SWOT matrix. The exercise will help the library director review everything that has been learned over the past nine months of collecting data and interviewing stakeholders, and it will also show if any additional information needs to be gathered before moving into the next stage of developing the integrated plan.

For strengths and weaknesses, the library director can list several things that came to light from assessments of the library. Positives include a collection that is well-developed and has many historic gems. The library building itself is well-designed and has a lot of natural light. The library staff is also a strength in that they are passionate, energetic professionals who are committed to serving the library's patrons. On the negative side of the matrix, the library has a small budget that makes it difficult to maintain collection development at pace with new publications. The library building and its physical plant systems are aging, which puts conservation of the collection at risk. The library staff are also overextended, and funding is not available to add positions and adjust workloads back to reasonable expectations.

For opportunities and threats, the library director learned quite a bit from researching the surrounding community and hosting conversations with stakeholders. On the positive side, there are several groups within the community that are finding a resonance with the library and its collection and services. The library's parent organization is extremely supportive and prepared to hear new ideas and fund reasonable new initiatives if possible. Negatively, the community is shrinking, which means that the patron base is also shrinking along with the pool of prospective donors. A global pandemic has also impacted circulation as patrons have shifted to more commercial means of satisfying their information needs: personal subscriptions to periodical publications, audiobook collections, and ebook collections, as well as direct purchases of books and other materials and services the library provides for circulation.

While the SWOT matrix is not perfectly balanced, the library director feels it accurately captures the strengths, weaknesses, opportunities, and threats of the Du Bois Library. Although the SWOT matrix does not yield many new insights, it is a good, visual method for recording and summarizing everything that has been learned through the months of research and assessment that is succinct and to the point. It forms the final piece of the Du Bois Library's analysis that will feed directly into their integrated plan, informing it so that the library can begin to build on its strengths and opportunities while dynamically responding to its weaknesses and threats.

Summary

Conducting research on your library, its immediate environment, and its surrounding communities is a critical first step for Integrated Library Planning.

This chapter detailed four primary types of research and analysis that are helpful when establishing an integrated plan. When engaging in these research activities, there may be a need to move fluidly between them instead of progressing through them in a linear fashion. Information learned later in a different research activity may lead to questions that require research methods explored earlier in the process. The process must be engaged in with healthy curiosity and flexibility so that these opportunities to go back and revisit earlier research methods and activities are recognized and taken. While a library may be excited and eager to move as quickly as possible into the development stage of the integrated plan, rushing the research stage will not only leave missed opportunities behind, it will also cripple the integrated plan.

Gathering background information involves researching three environments: the library itself, the library's immediate organization, and the library's surrounding community. It includes gathering facts and collecting historical material from past reports and documents. An institution's history may be recorded in published or unpublished sources, such as commemorative books or archived minutes from anniversary celebrations. The library's policies might already include some background and historical information. Previous planning documents may also have information that can be updated and built upon for the integrated plan.

The process for developing mission and vision statements is as much a research endeavor as it is a creative one. Mission and vision statements must be grounded in the library's situation, its relationships to its parent institution and the surrounding community, where it has been, and what it strives to become. Crafting and vetting these statements requires careful research and collaboration. Drafts of these statements need to be shared widely for feedback and reflection, then taken forward as research continues and revised as new insights emerge.

Conducting a comprehensive needs assessment is an important undertaking that will greatly inform the development of the integrated plan. It is a time-intensive research project that will take several months to complete. It includes all aspects of the library, from collections to services, from physical plant to online presence. There are a variety of methods that can be employed when conducting a needs assessment. This chapter explored analyzing statistics and usage patterns, collecting formal surveys and patron feedback, hosting conversations, and an adaptation of Appreciative Inquiry for Integrated Library Planning. Other methods for conducting a needs assessment may be added to or used as a substitution for any of the methods explored in this chapter if they are effective at researching and assessing needs across the library and its constituencies in an open, inclusive, and transparent way.

The final research and analysis activity to engage in before moving into developing the integrated plan is creating a SWOT matrix. This exercise summarizes and encapsulates all the gleanings from the research conducted, categorizing it according to its origin and the type of impact it has on the library. Organizing and synthesizing all that has been learned about the library into these four quadrants helps crystallize where the library is now, what assets it possesses, and what challenges it must work with. The SWOT matrix can also show where additional research or analysis might be needed if the balance of the quadrants is skewed in one direction.

When these four components are ready—background information, mission and vision statements, needs assessment, and SWOT matrix—work can then proceed to the next stage of the process. The foundation is now ready for building the structure of the library's integrated plan. The documents, information, and tools that have been gathered during this stage are essential to support the development and implementation of the integrated plan.

Preliminary: Pivoting toward an integrated future

Stage 1: Foundation and groundwork

Stage 2. Building a planning structure

Stage 3. Implementing a monthly review cycle

Stage 4. Long-term assessment and adjustment

CHAPTER 4

Building a Planning Structure

The second phase of Integrated Library Planning is building the planning structure. This creative process results in the construction of an organizational framework for ongoing library planning and management. This framework is built on the foundation of the background research and analysis conducted in the first phase and provides the overall structure for the monthly review cycle implemented in the third phase.

The planning structure has four levels (see figure 4). The top-most level contains the areas or divisions of library operations. Under each area are goals, the second level. Every goal has a set of strategic outcomes, the third level. And for each strategic outcome there are action plans, the fourth level.

The four levels of the planning structure can be represented in an outline format, hierarchical table, or web diagram. I find a web diagram to be the most useful because it visually presents the structure in a way that does not place one area of function in a higher priority over another (see figure 5). Mind mapping software can be extremely helpful in creating a web diagram. More information about using mind mapping software in Integrated Library Planning is included in appendix A.

While all the background information, research, and assessments collected during the first phase of the Integrated Library Planning process inform the development of the planning structure, the mission and vision statements are critical. This phase looks to the mission and vision statements as a summary and representation of all that the library is and strives to be. As a result, the goals,

52   Chapter 4

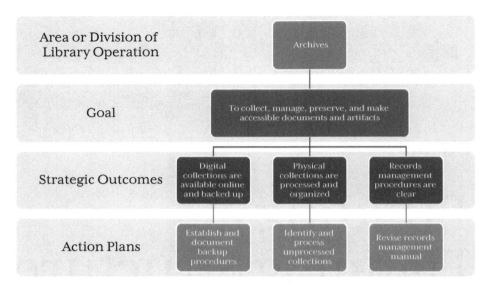

FIGURE 4
The four levels of the planning structure for an library's integrated plan.

FIGURE 5
An example of an integrated plan web diagram created with mind mapping software.

strategic outcomes, and action plans all stem from the mission and vision. Make sure that the mission and vision statements incorporate the sum of the background research and needs assessment and accurately reflect the library before moving forward.

Organizing Library Operations

Before any work can be done to create goals, strategic outcomes, and action plans, create a sketch of the library's organizational structure. The size and situation of the library will likely influence this part of the process. Larger libraries with larger staffs are likely to have already a very structured organization composed of departments and committees. Smaller libraries with small staffs or solo librarians may have more flexibility in defining areas and divisions for library operations. Libraries in a state of transition may find themselves questioning existing structures and wanting to create new ones. While situation and context may have heavy influence over the outcome, it is worth examining structures already in place and those under revision so that the goals, outcomes, and action plans that follow may be appropriately assigned for optimal growth and development toward the library's mission and vision.

Library operations encompass everything the library does. Operations include every aspect of information service, access, bibliography, conservation, education, curation, and public relations that a library engages in. Many libraries take a departmental approach to library operations, dividing them between specialized staff members and workspaces devoted to circulation, reference, cataloging, acquisitions, preservation, etc. For libraries that are already organized in such a way, it may make sense to retain this organizational structure for the integrated planning structure.

To determine whether the library's existing organizational structure is suitable for integrated planning, consider what was learned in the previous stage. How do the departments currently function? Does each department have sufficient staff and support? How is communication between departments? How well does the current work of each department match the new mission and vision statements?

The organizational structure of Integrated Library Planning will function differently in larger and smaller libraries. A larger library will likely have two or three operational areas whose staffs meet periodically and report to the chief administrator or administrative team of the library. In a smaller library, the two or three operational areas may or may not have a dedicated staff member to oversee the work of each area, much less meet independently to report to an administrative group. Regardless, it may yet be helpful for a small library to adopt a similar organizational structure as a larger library to be able to understand, prioritize, and assess the full scope of library operations.

Two or three operational areas is an optimal number for the Integrated Library Planning structure. If there are many operational areas, they may be grouped into divisions for more efficiency in the integrated plan. For example, a departmental structure may already exist in which the library operations are divided between public services and technical services. These two departments would become the two divisions of the planning structure. Within public services, however, are several more specific operational areas: circulation, reference services, programs, etc. Likewise, technical services may include cataloging, acquisitions, and collection development. While each individual operational area needs its own goals and strategic outcomes, the divisions of public services and technical services provide a layer of support and accountability within the planning structure, facilitating communication and innovation.

A library does not necessarily need to adopt the classic public services and technical services model for organizing library operations in the planning structure. New suggestions may have emerged in the process of gathering background information and crafting the mission and vision statements. In my small academic library, I used elements of the mission statement to organize the library's operations into three divisions. Our mission statement included commitments to scholarship, curiosity, and creativity. These three commitments became linked to three divisions: collections; learning, teaching, and research services; and resources. Each division combines more traditional areas of library operation and places them in relation to one another in a way that optimizes the Integrated Library Planning structure. For example, combined within the collections division are collection development, collection maintenance, and archives, which all support the library's mission to forward scholarship. Combined within the division for learning, teaching, and research are the library's instructional program and reference services, which support the library's mission to encourage curiosity. Combined within the resources division are outreach, spaces, and systems, which all support the library's mission to foster creativity.

By combining these eight operational areas into three divisions, their functions are linked by a core purpose. On a practical level, it is easier to map and assess the action plans of three main divisions rather than eight individual operational areas. On a functional level, the deeper connection between the operational areas of a division prompts cooperation, collegiality, and greater awareness of individual contributions to the whole. This type of organizational and planning structure prompts regular reflection on how the parts work together in the whole, particularly in the monthly review and assessment cycle.

The mission and vision statements, along with what was learned during the first phase, need to inform how library operations are organized in the planning structure. When a clear line can be drawn connecting the mission and vision

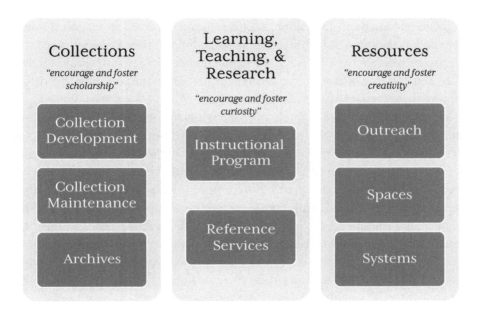

FIGURE 6
How operational areas were once organized at Lancaster Theological Seminary Library. Each division was linked to an aspect of the library's mission statement and contained operational areas for the integrated plan.

statements to the operational areas, it creates a strong foundation on which to build goals and strategic outcomes. Likewise, once the plan is in place the line must be traceable backward from action plan to strategic outcome to goal to mission and vision. Tracing these lines in an integrated plan helps keep progress toward outcomes and goals at the forefront and prompts adjustments in those goals and outcomes when new needs or conditions arise.

Case Study

Evers College Library is a mid-sized academic library with a full-time staff of fifteen including professional librarians and paraprofessional library assistants. It serves a college that grants several undergraduate degrees and offers a few master's degree programs in education, business, and the arts. At the time of starting the Integrated Library Planning process, the library was organized into departments for technical services, public services, and archives. Technical services included cataloging and metadata with library systems. Public services included reference and circulation. Archives oversaw the college's archival collections and a small rare book collection. In this configuration, there was very little overlap or collaboration between the departments. Library staff would interact with their colleagues in other departments, but most of the planning and visioning remained contained in each department.

During the first phase of Integrated Library Planning, Evers College Library staff members learn several things about the community the library seeks to serve. First, they learn that the library is already doing well serving the academic needs of Evers College students and faculty. The public services staff have developed some innovative educational programs to teach students how to navigate the library, receiving high marks in surveys for supporting the curriculum. Library staff members also learn that they could be doing more to meet the needs of college alumni. Graduates reported that they were often unaware of their library benefits as alumni. Those graduates who were regular library users, primarily from the master's programs in education and business, reported that the collection did not always meet their professional development needs.

Wanting to support the college's new initiatives in lifelong learning, Evers College Library crafts a new mission statement, focusing its work in two primary areas:

> *The mission of Evers College Library is to support and enrich the academic programs of Evers College and nurture a community of lifelong learners.*

Academic programs and a community of lifelong learners thus become the two primary areas that drive the library's operations. While the public services staff might be seen as those primarily responsible for carrying out the mission of the library, the library director understands the importance for all library staff to feel connected to the mission. This is not a goal or mission of one department. As the mission statement of the entire library, every member of the library's staff performing any function of the library needs to understand how they contribute to fulfilling this mission.

Taking a bold step, the library director begins the work of reorganizing the staff so that goals, strategic outcomes, and action plans align to the new mission statement. First, two divisions are established: academics and community. Next, each department is matched with a division that most closely aligns with its current work (see figure 7). Reference, cataloging, and metadata find a new home in academics. Circulation and archives find a new home in community. The work of library systems is split between the two divisions. Systems work related to electronic resource management finds a home in academics. Systems work related to the library's public-facing websites, marketing, and communication finds a home in community.

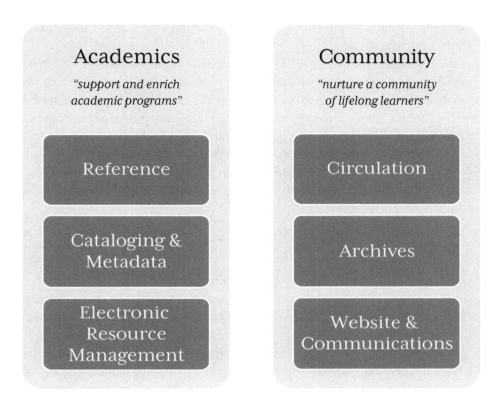

FIGURE 7
New divisions and department alignment for Evers College Library.

This new arrangement and distribution of library staff into two divisions has interesting results. It partners reference staff with cataloging and metadata staff, which strengthens and invigorates the library's much-loved educational programs. Having a systems librarian dedicated solely to electronic resource management and in regular communication and collaboration with reference and cataloging and metadata improves the library's electronic collections and the pathways by which to access it. Bringing circulation and archives together with a shared focus on nurturing a community of lifelong learners increases the visibility of alumni library benefits. Circulation staff are more intentional about reaching out to graduates when their library accounts are close to expiration. Archives staff help the library connect emotionally with graduates through social media posts and exhibits featuring events from the college's past. A systems librarian dedicated to website development and library communications proves to be key for planning and carrying out initiatives that bring both current students and alumni into the library.

Another pleasant outcome of this reorganization of staff for the integrated plan is that although they are arranged into two divisions, the integrated plan helps keep everyone connected and united under the library's mission statement. Staff members whose primary focus is on academic programs help support and participate in community activities, while staff members whose primary focus is on community help support and participate in academic activities. The new arrangement facilitates greater collaboration and innovation among library staff, who are now more engaged with the library's patrons. As a result, library usage and patron satisfaction climb upward.

Goals

Once library operations are organized into divisions and areas, it is time to set goals. A goal is a brief statement linking a specific function of an operational area to the library's mission and vision statements. Depending on how the divisions are structured, it may make sense to create goals for each operational area within a broader division. Goals ought to be short, concise, and relate to the general function of the operational area. I find "to" statements to be most effective for goals. For example, a goal for an operational area dedicated to collection maintenance could be: "To ensure that the collection is accessible and kept in good order."

When writing goals, consider the mission and vision statement in relation to each area or division. How does the operational area contribute to the library's mission? What is its unique contribution? How can the operational area help the library achieve its vision? Distill the answers to these questions into a "to" statement for each operational area.

Each operational area should have at least one goal. Some operational areas may need more than one. It is helpful at this level of the plan, however, to keep the number of goals low. It is easier to achieve this by keeping a general focus for each goal. As a link between the operational area and the library's mission and vision, a goal could also be understood as a statement of purpose. Why does this operational area exist? What does it do? How does it fit within the library's larger structure?

Goals need to be unique to each operational area. If there is any overlap between goals, this may be an indication that the organizational structure needs to be revisited. Similarly, if two operational areas have goals that are complementary to the point that they are heavily dependent upon one another, this might be an opportunity to consolidate or restructure divisions. Like the process engaged in the first phase, the process of establishing an organizational structure and creating goals can be fluid. The practice of writing goals may provide a different perspective on library organization, requiring tweaking of areas and divisions.

Once goals are prepared for each area or division, take a moment to review all the goals side by side. As mentioned earlier, arranging the goals visually in a web diagram can be helpful to get the "big picture" view of all the goals, how they relate to their divisions, relate to each other, and relate to the library's mission and vision statements (see figure 8). One comforting and somewhat innovative aspect of Integrated Library Planning is that these goals are not absolute. They are flexible and changeable. At any point during the planning process and in its implementation, a goal may be reevaluated and amended, eliminated, or replaced if it no longer serves its purpose or becomes obsolete. Suggestions about how to reevaluate and update goals are addressed in chapter six.

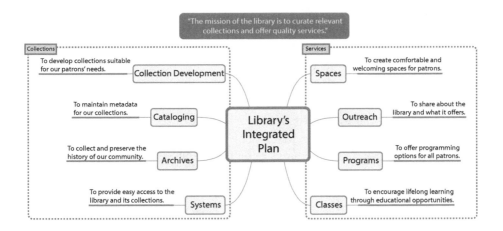

FIGURE 8
An example of how a web diagram can be used to show two divisions of operations with four operational areas each. Each operational area has a goal listed for it.
The library's mission statement is above the diagram. This type of visualization is helpful for reviewing all the goals in relation to one another and in relation to the library's mission statement.

Case Study

The mission of Freeman Memorial Hospital's library is "to promote health and empower knowledge-based learning for clinicians and patients." Corresponding to this mission, the library has arranged library operations into the following operational areas: print collections, electronic collections, customer service, and marketing. When setting goals for each of these operational areas, the librarian needs to connect each goal to the library's mission and inform it with what was learned during the research conducted in the first phase of developing the integrated plan.

The print collection is used primarily by clinicians studying for professional development courses and secondarily by patients' families who have questions about their loved ones' diagnoses and care. It needs to include current, relevant resources and to be arranged in a way that is user friendly for ready access. The goal the librarian sets for the print collection is "To curate a print collection of relevant, up-to-date resources arranged for ready access." The electronic collection is accessible from any computer in the hospital and is used mostly by doctors and nurses for research related to patient care. Since the needs and usage are slightly different from the print collection, the librarian creates a goal that reflects this: "To develop, maintain, and provide easy access to quality electronic resources." Both goals for print and electronic collections emphasize quality, up-to-date information and access, which is vitally important when promoting health and serving clinicians and patients who will be looking for the latest research and must be able to find it easily.

Customer service and marketing also have important roles in promoting health and empowering knowledge-based learning for clinicians and patients. Therefore, goals for these two operational areas also need to connect to the library's mission statement. Analysis of the library's reference transactions shows that clinicians and patients contacted the library staff through a variety of methods for research assistance. While some interactions were face-to-face, most reference transactions took place by phone or email. The goal the librarian creates for customer service reflects the need to offer service in a variety of modes: "To provide supportive and empowering library services via multiple modes, including in person and online." Since questions and requests come to the library through a variety of modes, the librarian sees the importance of marketing the library in the places where the clinicians and patients are: "To promote library resources that support health and learning throughout the hospital and its online portals." Each of these goals is specific to its corresponding area of library operations and wholly grounded in the library's mission statement.

Strategic Outcomes

Strategic outcomes are written and assigned to each goal as a way of transitioning from what the library aspires to do and what makes those aspirations possible. While goals generally address how each operational area and division helps the library to fulfill its mission and vision, strategic outcomes are more concrete and descriptive of how the goal may be achieved. They describe a state of being or result of the library's goal achievement. Strategic outcomes are the outward signs of the library's progress toward its goals, living into its mission, and bringing about its vision.

Each goal should have at least one strategic outcome and in most cases more than one strategic outcome. Where goals are general to the division or operational area in the library, strategic outcomes are more specific. For instance, strategic outcomes for the collection maintenance goal, "To ensure that the collection is accessible and kept in good order," may include specific statements relating to storage, preservation, inventory, and circulation.

Each layer of the planning structure becomes increasingly more specific. Strategic outcomes, layered between an operational area's general goals and the more practical action plans, need to have a balanced approach to details. Too little detail may result in ambiguity hindering the monthly review cycle. Too much detail may create a focus so narrow that it shuts out a wider perspective, making it difficult to map action plans effectively. When writing strategic outcomes, consider the goal and ask what signs or indicators would be present if the goal were being met. What would be the state of a division or operational area if the library is achieving its goal?

Strategic outcomes are flexible and changeable, just as goals are. They are regularly evaluated and assessed during the monthly review cycle. This is especially the case as the action plans associated with a strategic outcome are completed. Because of their nature, being more specific than a goal and directly connected with the action plans, strategic outcomes are revised more often than goals. The first attempt at identifying strategic outcomes is just that: a first attempt. It is a starting point. As the plan is implemented, it will become clear what tweaks to the outcomes might be needed.

Mapping External Standards to Goals and Outcomes

Fortunately, or unfortunately, many library directors are not able to manage and lead their libraries completely unchecked. There are governing bodies and overseers who often impose a set of standards on libraries and require regular reporting and assessment to ensure that these standards are being met. Academic libraries are bound by the standards set by their institution's accrediting agencies. Most states in the United States have established standards for their public libraries. School districts and state boards of education have standards for public school libraries. The major library associations in the United States also set forth their own standards, which are sometimes adopted by libraries and their governing bodies to guide operations.

Ensuring that the library is meeting standards placed on it by governing bodies and overseers can be an onerous process. For example, an academic library may go through a reaccreditation process once every eight or ten years, requiring the librarian to report specifically on how the library meets the standards set forth by the accrediting agency. Compiling this report is no small task and can often take a great deal of time and research. When external standards are considered during the planning stages of Integrated Library Planning, the work of compiling reports for governing bodies and overseers is streamlined.

To ensure that external standards are not driving the library's mission and vision, I recommend setting these standards aside during the first two-thirds of the planning structure phase. The way the library is organized, along with goal and strategic outcome development, should first reference the library's particular context, its stakeholders, and the needs of its users. This is always the primary focus and motivation for the library's planning and development. However, it can be helpful to bring external standards into conversation with the planning process once a first draft of goals and strategic outcomes is complete.

After the goals and strategic outcomes are drafted, compare them to the standards the library is asked to meet. For each standard, find the correlating goal and outcome. Sometimes the operational areas and divisions established early in this phase do not neatly align with external standards. Sometimes a standard applies to more than one area. As long as a connection can be made from each standard to a goal and its related strategic outcomes, the differences in the library's operational areas and the organizational structure of the standards do not matter. If there is a standard that cannot be mapped to a goal or strategic outcome within a goal, this may be an area of deficiency in the plan that ought to be addressed with further reflection and revision of the goals and strategic outcomes.

It will be helpful to record and keep track of the connections between the external standards and the integrated plan. There are several ways to do this. A spreadsheet or table can be used to list each standard and its corresponding goals and strategic outcomes. If goals and strategic outcomes are tracked with a web diagram, the corresponding standards can be added in a text box next to the diagram and connected with dashed or dotted lines if desired (see figure 9). This is a way to keep external standards present in the integrated plan without letting them drive the entire process. When the time comes to report on the library's operation in relation to these standards, the mapped connections become a helpful point of reference and guide. The monthly review report and assessment data can be easily collated and compiled into a report on standards required by the governing bodies and overseers.

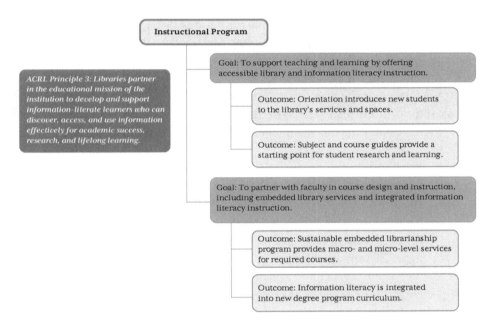

FIGURE 9
An example of how an external standard might be referenced within a library's integrated plan. Here, a principle from ACRL's *Standards for Libraries in Higher Education* (2011, rev. 2018) is referenced by the library's goals and strategic outcomes for its instructional program.

Case Study

The Shuttlesworth Theological Library serves an independent theological school accredited by the Association of Theological Schools (ATS). ATS issues the document *Standards of Accreditation*, to which all accredited theological schools must comply. The accreditation cycle is ten years since this theological school

64   Chapter 4

is maintaining its accreditation. A significant component of preparing for reaccreditation is completing a self-study report, to which all departments across the theological school contribute. Since ATS's sixth standard is solely for library and information services, the library director of Shuttlesworth Theological Library is tasked with compiling the information for this section of the self-study report.

While self-study and reaccreditation are several years away, the library director of Shuttlesworth Theological Library is already thinking about how the information needed for the self-study report will be collected and gathered when the time comes. The library director decides to integrate the ATS *Standards for Accreditation* into the goals and outcomes for the library's integrated plan. Taking this extra step at the beginning of the Integrated Library Planning process makes it easier to reuse and reorganize the information that is collected in monthly review reports for the self-study report.

The ATS *Standards for Accreditation* are not comprehensive of the operational areas and do not directly correlate to the areas and divisions that the library director has established for the integrated plan. For example, one standard reads:

> The library offers services that enhance student learning and
> formation and partners with faculty in teaching, learning,
> and research. Librarians provide reference services, help users
> navigate research resources, teach information literacy skills,
> support the scholarly and educational work of the school, and
> foster lifelong learning.

The library director created separate areas in the integrated plan for reference services and curriculum support and instruction. To map this standard to the integrated plan it must be shared between these two areas.

For the operational area that includes collection development, the library director finds two standards that apply (see figure 10). The first one relates to both curating collections and organizing them, which overlaps with the area that includes cataloging and metadata. The library director decides to include the standard in the charts for both collection development and cataloging so that it can be referenced in both areas.

In the case of systems, another area in the library's integrated plan, the only standard that could possibly match barely touches on the goals of this division:

> The library has sufficient financial, technological, and physi-
> cal resources to accomplish its purpose and to give equitable

attention and access to all the school's degree programs and modes of educational delivery.

This does not hamper Shuttlesworth Theological Library's goal for library systems to reach beyond sufficiency. The background research and preparatory work that provides a foundation for the library's integrated plan revealed a strength in adapting and implementing developing and bleeding-edge library technologies. Continuing to develop this strength for the benefit of the library's patrons is a goal for the systems area: "To utilize current and developing technologies to organize, manage, and maintain library data assets." Though utilizing current and developing technologies is different from what is required to provide sufficient technological resources, this strength of the library can be lifted up in the self-study by connecting it to this standard instead of adjusting the systems goal to better match the standard's requirements.

While the ATS *Standards of Accreditation* do not exactly match Shuttlesworth Theological Library's integrated plan, the library director finds value in mapping the standards for library and information services to the library's plan. The

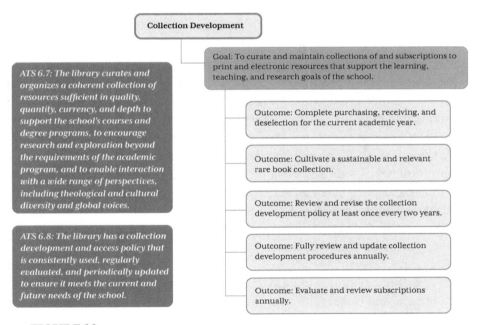

FIGURE 10
Shuttlesworth Theological Library's goal and strategic outcomes for collection development, which correlate with ATS standards 6.7 and 6.8.

process requires interpretation of the standards in relation to the integrated plan, as well as acknowledgement that the mapping process will not produce an exact fit in every instance. It is also helpful that the library director attempts to map the standards to the integrated plan at this stage, that is, once the goals and outcomes have already been drafted. In this way, the standards are a helpful gauge for the library to check that its integrated plan is sufficiently meeting the assessment needs of the school's accrediting body. At the same time, the goals and outcomes in the integrated plan are primarily informed by the library's background research, community conversations, and assessments instead of being influenced by the external standards, thereby leading to a more relevant and vibrant integrated plan.

Action Plans

At the most detailed level of the planning structure are action plans. These are the specific projects and actionable items that are necessary for the library to fulfill its mission and vision as depicted in the goals and strategic outcomes for each operational area. Action plans are very specific, include tasks assigned to staff, and have a set duration. This is the work of the library. Every service, project, task, and duty can be recorded as an action plan.

In significant ways, action plans in Integrated Library Planning have a much different function than action plans in a strategic plan. Strategic plans limit actionable items to those that directly pertain to the goals and strategic outcomes of the plan. Integrated Library Planning combines assessment with forward thinking and creates space for the ongoing essential tasks of the library to be considered alongside the needs of its users and future developments. In this way, the action plans created initially during this phase will likely include daily responsibilities as well as special projects, and they are all linked to strategic outcomes and goals. Every aspect of the library then becomes linked to the goals and strategic outcomes. Every staff person can see exactly how the work they are responsible for, both daily responsibilities and special projects, contributes to the library's mission and vision.

There are several different ways to approach compiling action plans for each strategic outcome. One way is methodically going through each strategic outcome and thinking through all the action plans that correlate with that outcome before moving to the next. Another way is to apply the "brain dump" strategy introduced by David Allen in *Getting Things Done*, a methodology of task organization and time management. This strategy encourages all possible tasks to be emptied out quickly into a list that can then be reviewed and sorted later. Decluttering the mind and recording everything without trying to match it with a strategic outcome can be very effective and efficient. Once all the tasks are recorded, then the work of sorting and assigning them to strategic outcomes

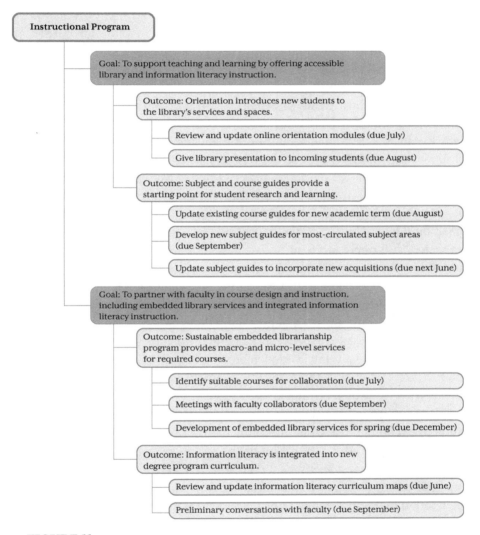

FIGURE 11
An example of how goals, strategic outcomes, and action plans for one operational area can be arranged in a tree-chart–styled web diagram. The same information could also be presented in a simple text-based outline. An advantage to using web diagram software instead of a word processor is the ability to click-and-drag items to reorder or rearrange them instead of using highlight, cut, and paste.

68   Chapter 4

may begin. Some tasks may be similar or related enough to be combined into one action plan while other tasks may stand alone as action plans. As everything is being sorted, gaps may become visible, inviting deeper thought and reflection on what action plans are missing among the strategic outcomes.

Action plans are the most detailed level of the planning structure, nested under strategic outcomes, and it is a good idea to list them in order of priority or sequence (see figure 11). If the planning structure is expressed in an outline format, the action plans can be grouped under a strategic outcome and nested in the outline structure by goal and then up to division or operational area. For planning structures expressed in web diagrams, the action plans may surround the strategic outcome in a way that visually represents their priority and sequencing. Regardless, some care must be taken to categorize and arrange the action plans according to which plans will be ongoing and the order in which plans should be pursued.

It may be helpful to think of the action plans created at this point as "starter" action plans. These are the action plans needed to get the integrated plan going. They represent basic steps to begin realizing the library's mission and vision. As the plan is implemented and work on these action plans commences, the need for adjustments or additional action plans may arise. These revisions are expected, and opportunity to update action plans is an important part of the monthly review cycle described in the next chapter.

Once a sufficient number of action plans have been created and organized under the strategic outcomes, the final organizational component is to begin scheduling the action plans and arranging them on the planning horizon. This exercise is the critical link between building the planning structure for the integrated plan and beginning its implementation. Scheduling action plans is an art that requires practice. Remember this so that you allow space for changes and flexibility as your plan is implemented.

First, go through the action plans and estimate how much time needs to be allowed to complete each one. There are many factors to consider when making this estimate. Will this action plan be the sole focus of a staff person, or will it be in progress alongside other action plans? What are the responsibilities of the staff person who will be working on this action plan and where does this specific plan fall in that staff person's priorities? As these estimates are being made, also consider the time of year when an action plan would be active. Is the plan linked with an activity or event that occurs at a specific time? Does it depend on information or resources supplied by someone external to the library's organizational structure? Any other information or contingencies to an action plan's completion is also important to note at this point.

Once all the action plans have estimates and notes attached to them, it is time to start placing them onto a timeline or calendar. I find arranging action plans visually to be tremendously helpful. A Gantt chart is often used to map projects with multiple stages and works very well for mapping action plans onto a timeline. There are several applications that can be used to create a Gantt chart, and these are included in appendix A. If a Gantt chart application seems too complicated to set up at this point, consider using a spreadsheet template. For those who prefer a more tactile mapping experience, draw the timeline on a white board or large sheet of paper posted to a bulletin board and then use self-adhesive notes for each action plan. The notes can be moved around on the timeline until the schedule is ready to be finalized.

Whether using a Gantt chart, other electronic chart, or a paper chart, the timeline will have the same basic structure. Because Integrated Library Planning operates on a rolling horizon, some thought as to the length of this rolling horizon is helpful at this point. It does not have to be the final decision, but this part of the planning provides an opportunity to try out a defined rolling horizon to see if it fits the library's needs (see figure 12). For some libraries, a twelve-month horizon is just the right length of time. For other libraries, twelve months is too short and they may prefer a fifteen- or eighteen-month horizon. Whatever length of time seems appropriate, lay out the months on the horizontal axis of the timeline or in the columns of a spreadsheet. The starting month should be the month when the integrated plan is expected to commence. Then, arrange the divisions or operational areas down the vertical axis of the chart or as rows

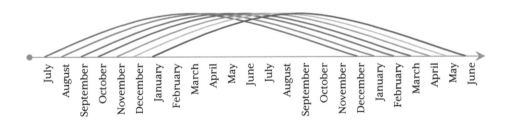

FIGURE 12
An illustration of how the rolling planning horizon works. The length of time depicted here is eighteen months. The first month's planning horizon begins in July of the current year and extends to December of the next year. When planning is revised the next month, the planning period will begin in August of the current year and extend to January of the year after next. The rolling planning horizon may be adjusted to suit any length of time, though fifteen- or eighteen-month periods are ideal for libraries with seasonal rhythms and activities that repeat annually and biennially.

of a spreadsheet. Once the basic structure is created, the action plans can then be placed according to operational area and under the ideal month or months each is anticipated to be active.

The first attempt at placing action plans on the timeline should consider the time of year an action plan would need to be active, its sequence or relationship with other action plans, and perhaps priority. Once all the action plans are on the timeline, it is likely that some parts of the timeline are more heavily scheduled than others. Therefore, a second look is necessary to create balance across the timeline. Anything that is not dependent upon a specific time of year could be moved into months that are less busy. When considering balance, it is also important to look at how work among the library's divisions and operational areas is balanced. Does each operational area have a consistent, steady flow of activity planned?

Balance across every operational area may not be the best option for every library. Depending on staffing structures and needs, it might be helpful for focus to shift from one operational area to another throughout the months, causing some areas to be rendered dormant periodically while action plans are pursued in other areas. Before finalizing the schedule of action plans, check again for any potential conflicts that might arise from staffing or external scheduling constraints. It is impossible to anticipate every possible conflict. Therefore, when possible, build in buffers. This way if something gets behind schedule it does not throw the entire plan into disarray.

You will be tempted to try to fit every action plan onto the timeline you have set, or to expand the timeline to accommodate all the action plans you have created. Resist these temptations. The nature of a rolling horizon is that it is perpetual. With each month that passes another month of planning is added to the end of the timeline. Action plans with lower priority or that cannot reasonably be scheduled at this point may go into a holding area to be added when an appropriate space appears on the rolling horizon. Action plans unassigned to the rolling horizon may continue to appear in the master integrated plan with a note indicating its status, "to be scheduled." Unscheduled action plans can then be tracked and regularly reviewed with the action plans that are scheduled on the rolling horizon.

Case Study

The C. H. Houston Public Library is nearly ready to implement its integrated plan. All that remains is to make a list of action plans and map them onto the rolling planning horizon. The library director asks all department heads to compile a list of current tasks and projects. These are shared during a brainstorming meeting and copied onto adhesive notes. The adhesive notes are then arranged onto a planning board that lists all the operational areas, goals, and strategic outcomes for the library's integrated plan.

At this point, the action plans on the planning board include everything that the library currently does or has in its immediate plans. Seeing them arranged on the planning board with the goals and strategic outcomes helps the planning team evaluate where additional action plans are needed. Together they review each strategic outcome and ask what action plans are necessary to realize that outcome. These are also jotted down on adhesive notes and added to the planning board.

When all the ideas for action plans are recorded on the planning board under a corresponding strategic outcome, the planning team then begins the work of determining priorities and timing. Action plans relating to seasonal activities, like the summer reading program, happen at the same time every year and are mapped onto the planning horizon accordingly. New initiatives, like digitizing the records of the town's chamber of commerce, may have more flexibility in timing based on the priority level of the project. The library director records everyone's ideas and input on the planning board since each department head brings a unique voice and perspective to the planning process.

After the brainstorming meeting, the library director maps the action plans onto the planning horizon. They enter everything from the planning board into a collaborative task management application that will help the library staff work together and communicate about the integrated plan once it is implemented. Each action plan is given a start and end date. These are transcribed onto a Gantt chart so that the library director can see how workloads are balanced. The first attempt at mapping the action plans shows that certain times of year are heavier than others. Summer, for example, is a busy time for special programs and this is also a time when staff typically want to take vacations. The library director adjusts the scheduling of action plans to accommodate these known rhythms of library activity.

Not all action plans fit onto the fifteen-month rolling horizon the planning team agreed upon. These action plans remain in the task management application without start and end dates assigned and are tagged so that they can be easily found and reviewed the next month. With the starter action plans mapped onto the planning horizon, the C. H. Houston Public Library is ready to implement its integrated plan. The library director feels assured about moving forward,

Summary

Building the planning structure for an integrated plan can be a creative, fun, and energizing process. The planning structure has four levels with the area and division of library operation at the top and goals, strategic outcomes, and action plans nested underneath. The process of building the planning structure is heavily informed by the background information, research, and assessments collected during the initial phase of the Integrated Library Planning process. The library's mission and vision statements guide the development of the planning structure as well as the crafting of goals and strategic outcomes.

A library engaging in Integrated Library Planning for the first time likely already has an organizational structure. This organizational structure may function well for the library and fit with its new mission and vision statements; in which case it would not need adjustment for an integrated plan. Some libraries may have an organizational structure that is modeled on older workflows, however, and would benefit from a review and reorganization. A suitable organizational structure for Integrated Library Planning consists of two to four main areas of operation. Each area has its own goals, strategic outcomes, and action plans. Some libraries may choose to have a larger number of more precise operational areas organized into divisions to develop and track more detailed goals and strategic outcomes. Therefore, adding another layer to the organizational structure is a way to allow for more precise assessment while also creating efficiency by grouping related operational areas into larger divisions. Libraries are free to be creative in defining operational areas and divisions to reflect the library's mission and vision: what the library does and what it aspires to be.

Once the organizational structure is in place, the process of writing goals may begin. Goals are best written as concise "to" statements. It should also be clear how a goal directly relates to the library's mission and vision statement. This does not necessarily mean that every goal needs to echo a portion of the mission or vision statement. Rather, a well-written goal should be an answer to the question "What contribution does this division or area of library operation make to the library's mission?" Every division or area will have at least one goal, though it is acceptable to have more than one. Looking at all the goals when they are drafted helps give a sense of the whole of library operations and how each division or area contributes to the mission. Any overlaps or gaps that emerge at this point are a prompt to go back and revise the goals.

When goals are in place, strategic outcomes are written to accompany them. There is some parallel between strategic outcomes and the vision statement in that a strategic outcome describes a state of being that will exist when progress is made toward the goal. Each goal will have at least one strategic outcome, oftentimes multiple outcomes. It is helpful to include some detail in strategic outcomes, but too much detail may hinder the development of effective action plans; therefore, writing strategic outcomes calls for a balanced approach. Goals and outcomes may be revised at any point during the life of an integrated plan. The strategic outcomes and goals written at this point in the process should be considered a starting point and not something to belabor in pursuit of perfection.

If the library is required to adhere to a set of external standards, it may be helpful to link those standards to the integrated plan as the planning structure is being built. This serves to shape the library's integrated plan and monthly review process so that it may be used to inform assessments and reports related to the external standards. Care needs to be taken while doing this, however. It is important that an integrated plan reflect the needs, strengths, and aspirations of the library. External standards can be a helpful reminder of what needs to be considered but should not be the primary influence on a library's integrated plan. An ideal time to consider external standards and map them to the integrated plan is after the goals and strategic outcomes have been drafted.

When the strategic outcomes are complete, action plans may be written and organized appropriately. An integrated plan is most effective when encompassing all aspects of library operation. To achieve this, action plans should include special projects and initiatives along with day-to-day operations. By including both, the integrated planning process offers a holistic approach to library leadership and management and provides opportunities to innovate and discover efficiencies for both daily operation and special projects. One of the most effective ways to begin compiling action plans for the integrated plan is to begin making a list, preferably as a brainstorm with library staff. Once all the action plans are compiled in a list, they can then be assigned to the most appropriate strategic outcome. Any action plan that does not correlate with an outcome provides an opportunity to revisit the outcomes, the action plan, or both. As action plans are distributed to the strategic outcomes, they are given a place on the rolling planning horizon. This is usually a careful process that involves reviewing workloads and striving for balance while considering the rhythms of the library's year. As with goals and strategic outcomes, action plans and their placement on the rolling horizon are not absolute and unmovable. Once the integrated plan is implemented, all these pieces are reviewed and assessed on a regular cycle, to be revised or updated as needed.

At this point, the preparation for an integrated plan is complete. The library's operations are organized into operational areas, each with at least one goal, and strategic outcomes identified for each goal. The strategic outcomes have been broken down into tangible and measurable action plans which have been scheduled onto a timeline. Everything is now prepared for the implementation of the library's integrated plan.

Preliminary: Pivoting toward an integrated future
Stage 1: Foundation and groundwork
Stage 2. Building a planning structure
 Stage 3. Implementing a monthly review cycle
Stage 4. Long-term assessment and adjustment

CHAPTER 5

Implementing a Monthly Review Cycle

It has taken a lot of preparation and planning to get to this point: implementation. The work of the first two phases has probably taken at least six months, perhaps more. Implementation is the transition from the preparation and planning into doing the work of fully integrated operation, assessment, and strategic decision-making.

Implementation of Integrated Library Planning hinges on the establishment of a monthly review cycle. Essentially, the review cycle is a routine that top-level management oversees, keeping the integrated plan moving forward on its rolling horizon. The monthly review cycle has three primary objectives: facilitating communication, routinizing assessment, and planning forward. In the pursuit of these objectives, information is gathered and processed in a monthly review report, which records the library's progress toward goals and strategic outcomes, assesses action plans, evaluates financial positions, and considers observed information needs. The monthly review cycle offers the opportunity to continue collecting data and reviewing observations to inform ongoing assessment of the library's work. Adjustments to action plans, strategic outcomes, and goals are sometimes the result of this ongoing review and assessment.

Initial implementation of a monthly review cycle may not be smooth. It may take several months to find a rhythm that suits the entire staff and the library administrator's leadership style. This chapter begins with an overview of the monthly review cycle and then describes the elements of a monthly review report in detail. It closes with suggestions for customizing the review cycle and report for a library's particular context and situation.

Overview of the Monthly Review Cycle

The monthly review cycle is a workflow of practices established to keep the library's integrated plan in motion. Its objectives are to maintain and enhance communication among staff and management; to assess the library's ongoing work, financial situation, and progress toward strategic outcomes and goals; and to incorporate new insights into the plan while moving the rolling horizon forward. These objectives are pursued through a combination of meetings and activities. While these practices may add to the work already being done in the library, the benefit is worthwhile. Constant communication, continual assessment, and timely planning increase the overall efficiency and effectiveness of the library.

Your library may already include versions of the meetings and activities described here. Perhaps they are not approached with the same objectives in mind, or perhaps the activities are not engaged as frequently as they are in the monthly review cycle. Nevertheless, if similar practices or routines already exist in your library, it may be possible to simply adapt them to fit the needs of the monthly review cycle. Modifying existing practices can help ease the transition into an integrated plan and alleviate anxiety among staff who fear there will be more work or more time spent in meetings.

The standard monthly review cycle takes place over the course of a month and repeats each month. It is comprised of three primary activities:

1. reviewing and assessing library operations, particularly progress made toward strategic outcomes and goals and the status of each operational area;
2. reconciling the library's finances; and,
3. collecting and analyzing data on information needs and behavior to identify emerging trends and issues that impact the library and its patrons (see figure 13).

The beginning of the month is spent transitioning from the previous month to the new month. During this phase the monthly review report for the previous month is drafted, shared, and discussed with staff, and then finalized. In preparation for the month ahead, management discusses with library staff any

FIGURE 13
The three activities that make up the monthly review cycle. These three activities facilitate communication, assessment, and planning—the three objectives of the monthly review cycle.

currently active projects and what might be achieved during the month ahead. Throughout the month, progress is monitored. The style and manner of these progress checks depends on the size of a library's staff. Larger libraries may hold separate departmental meetings throughout the middle of the month, while smaller libraries with a sole administrator may review the status of the plan once in the middle of the month. As the month ends, assessments, financial reconciliation, and information behavior analysis are collected into the draft of the monthly review report. As the months transition, the cycle repeats.

Simply carrying out these activities each month is not enough to realize the full potential of Integrated Library Planning. The activities feeding information into the monthly review report must be pursued with the primary objectives in mind: strong and healthy communication among library staff members, routinizing assessment in a way that promotes curiosity and engagement with what is going on both within the library and around it, and perpetual planning that maintains a forward momentum. Appreciating how each objective supports the plan will enable a smooth and successful implementation.

Communication

Good communication is essential to the function of any organization. The health of an organization can often be assessed by the quality of communication among staff, management, and administration. Integrated Library Planning relies on two-way communication. Staff keep management informed of progress and new developments while management keep staff informed of the library's overall status and changes to the integrated plan.

It is important for the work environment to promote good communication. Just as a library's reference desk or circulation desk may invite questions and interaction with patrons, so may individual work environments for staff. Both may be approached with a similar philosophy. This is not to encourage constant chatter and interruption, but individual staff members may want to think about how they can nonverbally communicate to their colleagues that they may be interrupted or approached with a question. Some staff may prefer a phone call first. Others may prefer an email or chat prompt. For staff members who do not mind being approached in person first, some kind of visual on the desk or a sign on the door to indicate when they are available to be interrupted may be helpful. Each person has their own working style, and spending some time in staff development to learn and how best to interact can be a valuable exercise. For staffs that include part-time employees, employees who work nontraditional hours, and employees who work in a hybrid or remote environment, there are several technologies available to stay connected with one another synchronously and asynchronously.

Informal communication resulting from spontaneous or impromptu conversations between staff is only a small piece of facilitating communication in the library. Under Integrated Library Planning, it is important to have formal meetings with agendas and objectives, held at regular intervals. These meetings, when run efficiently, can keep the work of the integrated plan moving forward. The number and type of meetings required for a monthly review cycle depends on the size and configuration of the staff.

Consider the following approach for a mid-sized library with a plan organized by two or three major divisions, each division containing multiple, more specific areas. Each division, chaired by a department manager or leading staff member, convenes a monthly meeting of all the staff in that division. That meeting takes place in the middle of the month when the previous month's report is released. Any overall progress or important information from the library director is shared with the staff. Each staff member has an opportunity to share progress on projects and action plans as well as any observations and questions relevant to the work of the division. The division leader compiles the progress reports, observations, and unanswered questions from the division staff into a report. Each division leader then brings their report to a meeting of division leaders and the library director. This meeting takes place in the last week of the month or the first week of the new month. A draft of the monthly library review report is discussed, and the director leads a conversation among the division leaders to analyze the information collected from each division and to determine if changes to the plan are needed. If a change is not needed now, a watch list is compiled to see if new observations become trends that may necessitate a future change.

One strategy to make these meetings more successful and efficient is the compilation of pre-read reports. Simply put, this strategy requires each participant in the meeting to compile a written report of what they are responsible for sharing in the meeting, distribute that report ahead of time to everyone involved in the meeting, and arrive at the meeting prepared to discuss everyone else's report. When pre-read reports are shared and read by everyone in advance, meetings can run much more efficiently because time is spent on discussing the reports instead of simply reporting. On the surface, it is a commonsense strategy that many would have practiced in school to prepare for class. However, it is a strategy that takes a great deal of trust and commitment from everyone in the meeting. It requires that everyone commit to completing and sharing their reports on an agreed upon date so that everyone has sufficient time to review documents prior to the meeting. It also requires commitment from the library director and division leaders to make sure that staff members have time to compile and read the reports. These reports do not have to be long and detailed; a few paragraphs or single page is usually sufficient.

Library leadership is at the core of fostering healthy communication practices among library staff. Without the commitment, trust, and positive role modeling of the library director and other leaders, it is very difficult to establish the communications practices needed to make Integrated Library Planning successful.

Assessment

Regular, ongoing assessment is the second objective of the monthly review cycle. Assessment has become a buzz word in management, including library management. How do we know what we do is working effectively and successfully? By sound assessment practices, of course. The more important question, however, is not "Are we successful?" but "How do we effectively measure our performance?"

80   Chapter 5

At its core, assessment is data collection and analysis at its core. Good assessment requires library leaders to turn into researchers. Just as good research practices demand the researcher attempt to remain impartial and open to unexpected outcomes, good assessment practices must also remain objective. The purpose of assessment is not to prove that a course of action or solution is successful. Its purpose is to evaluate the outcomes of a course of action and then to analyze those outcomes in relation to what is desired and needed.

The most familiar and popular mode of library assessment is quantitative statistical data. Many libraries collect statistical data on a wide range of library functions: circulation, acquisitions, cataloging, interlibrary loan, and electronic resource use, to name a few examples. Depending on the nature of the action plans, these statistics can form a firm foundation for assessment. Other types of statistics that might be helpful are reference inquiries, website traffic, and search terms.

Assessment is more than simply collecting and reporting statistics, however. It also involves analysis of that data *vis-à-vis* the library's goals, outcomes, and action plans. Sometimes quantitative data needs to be combined with qualitative data, such as narratives collected from staff and library users, to assess whether a particular action is having the desired impact on goals and outcomes. For example, to assess an embedded librarian program it would be helpful to survey the embedded librarian, the instructor, and the students in the course. It would also be helpful to review circulation, keyword search terms, and electronic resource usage data for time periods in the course when the students were actively engaged in research. By combining the statistical data with the survey results, a clearer picture of the embedded librarian's impact on the students' research practices emerges. Were searches more productive? Did circulation increase? Did the instructor report higher quality research from students? Was the student research experience improved? These assessment questions can be answered more fully when both quantitative and qualitative data are analyzed together.

Planning

Planning is the third objective of the monthly review cycle. The rolling horizon feature of Integrated Library Planning demands that the library administrators always be thinking ahead and moving the plan forward. However, planning is more complex than simply tacking additional projects and action plans to the end of the perpetually moving planning horizon. As the library's integrated plan is implemented, adjustments to the plan are inevitable. Changes to planning are also influenced by what is learned from communication and assessment throughout the month.

First, consider how planning is tracked. A Gantt chart is invaluable when scheduling action plans and mapping them onto the integrated plan's rolling horizon (see figure 14). To create a Gantt chart, the action plans are arranged onto a horizontal timeline. The timeline is measured by a set unit of time, usually weeks or months. The sample chart in figure 14 uses months. An action plan is represented as a colored bar spanning the expected timeframe. For an added layer of detail, the bars may be color coded according to an action plan's operational area and division or according to the staff member responsible for overseeing the project. Gantt charts are extremely helpful in visualizing how action plans are distributed across the planning period as well as across the library's functional areas. Ideally, library leadership looks for balance across both the planning period and the operational areas.

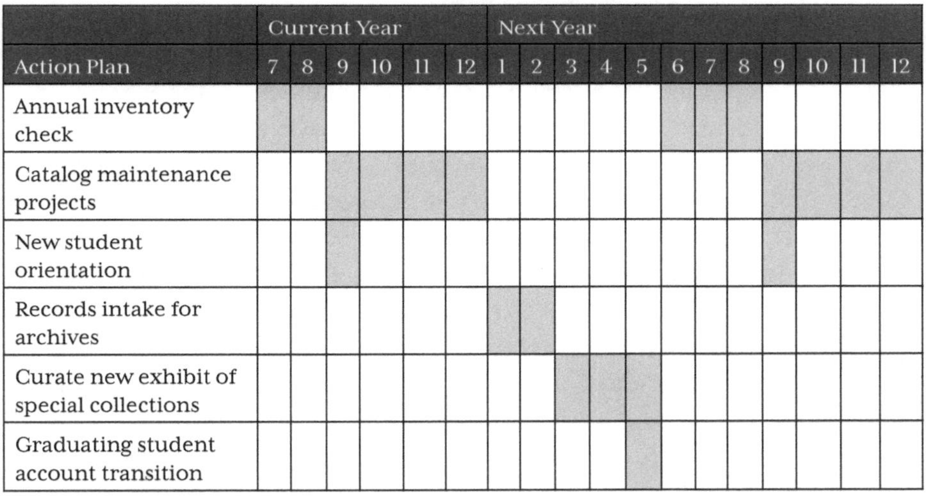

Action Plan	Current Year						Next Year											
	7	8	9	10	11	12	1	2	3	4	5	6	7	8	9	10	11	12
Annual inventory check	▓										▓							
Catalog maintenance projects			▓	▓	▓										▓			
New student orientation			▓												▓			
Records intake for archives						▓												
Curate new exhibit of special collections								▓	▓									
Graduating student account transition											▓							

FIGURE 14

A simple Gantt chart example created using a spreadsheet. The same row can be used to visualize repeating actions, such as the annual inventory check in the example above.

Timing action plans with the events and rhythms of the library and its users is one important consideration when looking for balance in planning. In an academic library, there are certain tasks and demands that can be anticipated based on the academic calendar. In a public library, holidays and seasons impact when and how some action plans are addressed. These rhythms are important to remember when scheduling action plans. When times in the planning period are filled with essential and high-priority action items, temporarily suspending or rescheduling nonessential action plans for less hectic times in the planning period can enhance productivity and efficiency while creating a better sense of balance. Busy and stressful periods when all available resources are taxed to maximum capacity are unavoidable. Being able to identify and anticipate when these periods will arrive within the planning period is an extremely important step toward achieving balance.

Distributing action plans equally among the library's operational areas and divisions is also important. Available human resources are a crucial consideration when determining the planning schedule. In libraries with multiple departmental staff, this may not be as much of an issue. For smaller libraries with staff who oversee multiple functions and tasks within the library, care must be taken not to overburden staff members. Again, balance must be sought if library staff are to fulfill expectations of productivity. Understanding when staff may be taxed with time-sensitive responsibilities enables the library administrator to schedule time-independent action plans when staff are not already occupied.

Another important consideration is grouping and sequencing action plans to maximize efficiency. No one likes to revisit a task or redo work that had been done in the recent past. With a planning horizon that is perpetually moving forward, there is a long planning field in which action plans can be reordered and rearranged when need arises. Unforeseen complications, staffing changes, emerging needs, or financial considerations may alter the plan. In all of these cases, being able to step back and review how the action plans fit together in the whole of the integrated plan is important. It allows library leaders to view planning on micro and macro levels, making sensible and timely adjustments based on available information.

Basic Components of the Monthly Review Report

The product of the monthly review cycle is a monthly review report. These reports serve as a record for the library's integrated plan and may be revisited from time to time as needed. These reports may also serve to communicate to administrators, overseers, and select stakeholders outside of the library's staff the progress being made in the library toward goals and outcomes. Each month, the integrated plan is revised and reaffirmed through the monthly review report. It is the living document that is carried forward once the plan is implemented.

The monthly review report flows directly out of the communication, assessment, and planning taking place throughout the month. In some ways, the monthly review report provides a structure for communication, assessment, and planning practices. The best way for the monthly review cycle and monthly review report to function, however, is for them to inform each other. There are certain things that need to be included in the monthly review report. A few are described in the subsections below, and there may be additional items to include relevant to your library's context and the audience of the report. As library administration engages in the monthly review cycle, further development of the monthly review report will likely follow. The goal is for the monthly review cycle and production of the monthly review report to become a dynamic process based on what helps the library best respond to emerging trends and needs.

Although your monthly review report will look slightly different based on your library's context, there is a standard outline that provides a helpful starting point. The basic components of the monthly review report are: progress assessments for each operational area of the library; financial summary; information needs and behavior analysis; and integrated planning updates to goals, strategic outcomes, and planning charts (see figure 15). Cumulatively, the information in these sections provides a comprehensive snapshot of the library and its operations at a particular moment in the integrated plan. The practice of creating the report brings emerging trends to light. Sample outlines for the monthly review report are found in appendix B. Each component of the monthly review report is detailed below.

Content for the Monthly Review Report

Assessment of Progress:	Financial Summary:	Information Needs and Behavior Analysis:	Integrated Plan Updates:
• Section for each operational area • Status of action plans • Progress toward strategic outcomes	• Summary of expenditures and receipts • Budget overview	• Quantitative data • Qualitative data • Emerging trends • Watch list	• Mission and vision statements • Goals and strategic outcomes • Rolling horizon planning charts

FIGURE 15

An outline of content that goes into a monthly review report. This content can be arranged and presented in a variety of ways depending on what works best for the library and the report's audience.

Assessment of Progress

Once the library's integrated plan is implemented, a helpful place to start is assessing the progress of action plans toward goals and outcomes. Each active action plan in each operational area of the library is examined and reported on. Is the action plan on track for completion in the expected time frame? For action plans that are ongoing or do not have a time frame, is the work being done still meeting the library's goals? When assessing the progress of action plans, the need for adjustment is not uncommon. Therefore, the monthly review report records not only the status of action plans, but also additions, deletions, and revisions.

Many libraries may also choose to monitor ongoing tasks in the monthly review report. Acquisitions, cataloging, shelving, book repair, interlibrary loan requests, and other routine work may find a home in the monthly review report. By including these tasks in the integrated plan and by monitoring them in the monthly review report, they are tracked as vital functions of the library. In the monthly review report, statistics and other data may be included to represent the ongoing work and dedication of resources to these perpetual tasks. Over time, patterns may emerge to better assist library administrators in scheduling action plans in concert with the routine work vital to the library.

The assessment section of the monthly review report mirrors how the library is organized in the integrated plan. Each operational area and division may have its own page or subsection. Using the same order and format each month keeps the report organized. A brief summary or bullet point list of what was accomplished that month and what adjustments were made is usually all that is necessary. Another approach is to create a dashboard. A dashboard is a way to visualize the status of each operational area of your library. If an application or tool is being used to track action plans, screenshots from that application could become elements of the dashboard. Thoughts and questions recorded in the monthly review report can also be tracked on the dashboard and revisited in later months. This visualization is often very helpful in making additions or adjustments to the plan. Including a planning chart or rolling horizon timeline as part of a dashboard is also extremely helpful.

Financial Summary

Many of the library's goals and outcomes cannot be achieved without proper funding. The financial summary is a crucial piece of the monthly review report. A clear understanding of the financial health of the library aids the library administrator in evaluating what financial resources might be needed to fund new initiatives prompted by emerging needs. On the surface a financial summary is simply a report of expenditures and income for the month. On a deeper level, however, it is the product of tracking and analyzing cash flow through the library's budget. Depending on the report's audience, library administrators may or may not choose to divulge all available financial details in the monthly review report. Regardless, there are three main points to look at when examining library finances during the monthly review.

The first point is financial reconciliation. This is especially important for libraries that exist within another institution with a centralized business office. Every library should have a method of tracking everyday expenditures. This could be handled through the integrated library system, a specialized acquisitions system, or perhaps through a spreadsheet. When there is a second accounting system in place, like that of an institutional business office, it is important to reconcile the library's internal records with the business office's account ledgers. For libraries that operate independently, financial reconciliation occurs with the library's bank statements. Reconciliation, the process of comparing and verifying that all transactions between the library's internal records and financial records kept by an outside entity match, is essential for sound financial management of the library. It also ensures that library administrators have the most accurate information about the library's finances when making decisions in the integrated plan.

The second point is reviewing expenditures within the context of the annual budget. Of primary importance is asking "Is spending on budget?" A quick look at balances will usually provide a yes or no answer. It is often important to look deeper than this, though. Library spending ebbs and flows with the rhythm of subscriptions and service contracts. A one-month glance at spending and balances in the library's budget cannot show whether spending is truly on target. Forward thinking is necessary to consider money that may already be committed to certain expenses. Once those amounts are calculated into the library's overall expenditures, spending can be assessed more fully. If a budget surplus is expected, Integrated Library Planning can effectively identify the top priorities that might benefit from additional financial investment. If a budget deficit is expected, Integrated Library Planning can help identify strategic cuts to reduce or eliminate deficit spending.

The third point is reviewing sources of income within the context of the annual budget. This will vary greatly by library context; however, many libraries track income to help cover expenses. Sources of income might include copies and printing, late and lost item fees, membership fees, merchandise sales, and donations. Helpful questions to ask about these sources of income are: What percentage of expenditures is covered by income? Is income steady, growing, or declining? How is income used in the current budget? How could income impact a future budget? These are all important factors to consider within the scope of Integrated Library Planning. Understanding the complete picture of expenses and income helps administrators plan for the future.

Information Needs and Behavior Analysis

Just as the foundation and groundwork phase involves assessing information needs and collecting observations of patron information behavior, the monthly review report records ongoing observation and analysis of information needs and behavior. This is one of the primary benefits of Integrated Library Planning: it creates space for ongoing observation and analysis so that emerging trends may be acted upon in a strategic and timely manner. While action plans are being carried out, library staff are also staying attuned to what is going on in the library and how patrons are engaging with the library, its services, and its collections. There are two main types of data collected for this section: quantitative statistics and qualitative observations.

While some quantitative statistics may be included in the assessment sections for each operational area, additional statistics may be helpful in this section of the monthly review report. For example, statistics showing the number of checkouts, renewals, and local use in the most recent month compared to previous months is helpful for assessing the library's circulation activity. Circulation statistics broken down by patron type, however, are more useful for detecting information needs and analyzing information behavior. Are some types of patrons using the library more than others? Is there a steady decline in library use among one group of patrons, indicating actions needed to improve service to that user population? Other statistics not included in the assessment portion of the monthly review report that may be helpful here are circulation statistics by call number, top search terms recorded by the library's catalog, and most asked reference questions.

Qualitative observation is often more ambiguous and fluid, but no less important than quantitative statistics. A good place to begin is sharing general observations about library use and patron information behavior during staff meetings. These informal observations often lead to more formal lines of inquiry and research into information needs. For example, a staff member may observe patrons having difficulty utilizing public computers, raising a concern about functionality and ease of use for patrons. Agreeing that this is worth looking into, library staff commit to more intentional observations of patrons when they are using the computers. A survey instrument might be developed and made available to patrons when they are using the public computers. As these additional observations are collected and analyzed, needs begin to emerge that can be addressed with the development of new action plans incorporated into the rolling horizon. Qualitative observation can extend beyond direct observations of patrons in the library. It also includes monitoring patron interaction with the library's social media presence, as well as patron comments and feedback on external websites that offer ratings and review services, like directories of community businesses.

Some data collecting activities are good to keep on a monthly schedule. Others may ebb and flow with the rhythms of the library and the community. Most quantitative statistics are easy to collect and analyze on a monthly basis. It is also a good idea to create space for sharing qualitative observations on a monthly basis, but these observations may not always lead to deeper research. It may be helpful to repeat some qualitative research on a regular schedule, such as a perennial survey on library services or reference interactions. Because these types of surveys are often time intensive, include their design and administration of them in the integrated plan.

Recording and reporting data is not enough; you must also analyze it. How does this month's data compare to last month's? What might be the reasons for change? Do we have enough information to add any actionable items to the integrated plan? If so, what is the priority, what additional steps are necessary to fit new action plans onto the rolling horizon? These are all critical questions when it comes to analyzing data on patron information behavior and identifying emerging information needs. At times, the data collected prompts questions encouraging reflection on trends beyond the library. Are there any unexplained trends developing? What are things that we should watch for and questions we could investigate over the coming months? This part of the monthly review cycle and report is also an opportunity to explore larger dynamics and developments impacting the library and its users.

Integrated Plan Updates

This is the point in the monthly review report where the focus shifts from the past month toward the month ahead. Any goals and strategic outcomes revised as a result of the monthly review cycle are noted in this section. There may be several months at a time when there are no changes or adjustments to goals and strategic outcomes. Action plans see the most activity and change, and these changes are included in the earlier assessment portion of the monthly review report. Changes to goals and strategic outcomes are usually prompted by larger events or dynamics. For instance, when all action plans under a strategic outcome are completed the outcome may be reviewed. If the library administrator finds the strategic outcome has been achieved, a new strategic outcome may be crafted to replace it.

Changes to goals and strategic outcomes are noted in this section, usually accompanied by a brief explanation or rationale for the change. If goals and strategic outcomes are visually presented in a chart or outline, include an updated version of the entire set for reference purposes. If no changes are made to goals and strategic outcomes, include the entire set here for reference anyway. It serves as a reminder that these pieces of the integrated plan are not static but are meant to be a living part of the library's planning rhythms. New knowledge emerging from the integrated planning process informs the goals and strategic outcomes. Recalling them every month and reviewing their relevance is an important component of the monthly review cycle.

Updated planning charts for action plans may also be included in this section, especially if they are not included as part of a dashboard in the assessment sections. As mentioned earlier, I prefer to map action plans on the rolling horizon using Gantt charts. Planning charts compiled and included here serve as a reference point for the month ahead. In the process of creating and compiling the monthly review report, it is likely that many action plans were rearranged and rescheduled. Unless it is particularly helpful, it is not necessary to indicate specific changes to the planning charts. The reasons for changes usually are named in the assessment portion of the report. In most cases the planning charts for action plans simply show the planning for the period of the rolling horizon (e.g., eighteen months).

Depending on the library's staff size and the audience for the monthly review report, it may also be helpful to include planning charts in two formats. One set of planning charts would show action plans organized by operational area. Another set of planning charts would show action plans organized by staff member. Including both sets of charts helps library administrators and staff visualize the sequence of action plans within the library's operational areas and divisions, as well as visualize workload for individual staff members.

Customizing the Monthly Review Cycle

The monthly review cycle has tremendous flexibility to accommodate a library's size, staff, and institutional structure. An implementation might have all the elements described in this chapter, executed and repeated monthly. This is not optimal for every shape and size of library. How can you customize the monthly review cycle to best fit your library's needs? The basic steps are to compare your library's current working rhythms with the ideal monthly review cycle, ask key questions about what is realistic for your library and its staff regarding meeting the objectives of the monthly review cycle, and then try modifying the cycle to blend current rhythms with the practices introduced by Integrated Library Planning.

A library's integrated plan can be monitored and executed by a team of library administrators, for example, a library director assisted by two or more managers. This team of administrators meets separately with library staff in each operational area during the month and reports progress and findings at an integrated planning meeting as one month transitions to the next. The outcome of these planning meetings is the monthly library review report, which is then shared at the next round of operational area meetings. The process looks like this (see figure 16):

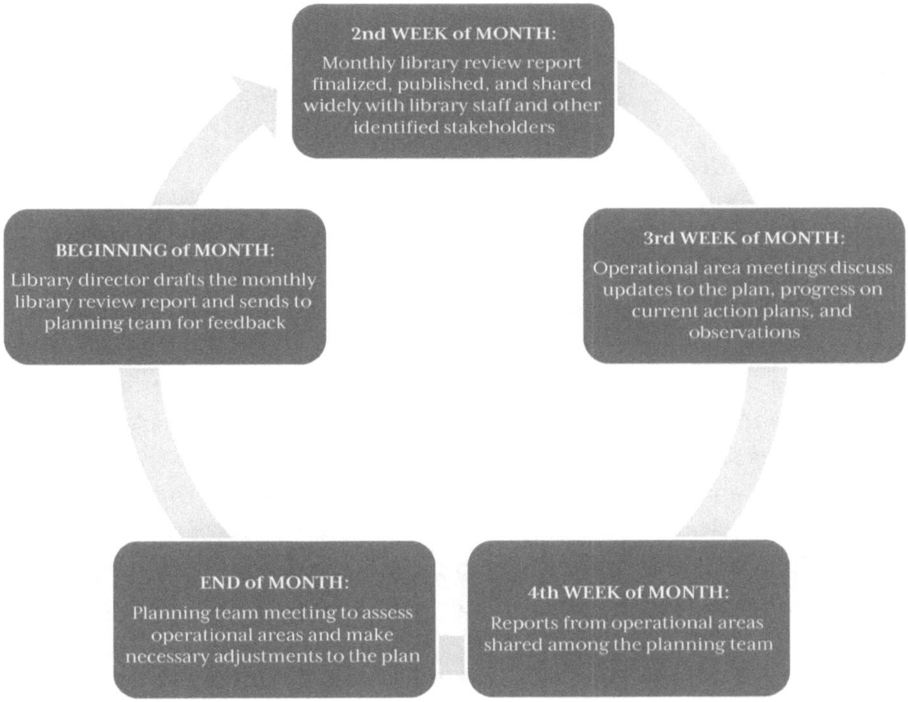

FIGURE 16
The monthly review cycle and the activities that are engaged in during each week of the month.

The objectives of the monthly review cycle are fully met in this process. The cyclical rhythm of assessment and analysis provides a structure for clear two-way communication between library staff and library administrators. The operational area meetings provide a place for staff to hear what was decided by the planning team and to contribute feedback and observations to administrators. The planning team meetings provide a place for administrators to hear the feedback of library staff and to discuss how to incorporate that feedback into the plan as the rolling planning horizon moves forward. Assessment happens on both the staff level and the administrative level as the operational area reports and monthly library review report are prepared. This process also provides space for regular and consistent planning. The planning team spends focused time in its meeting to review planning charts, adjust scheduled action plans, and make further amendments to goals and strategic outcomes.

A team approach to the monthly review cycle is best suited for larger libraries with a hierarchical staffing structure and some measure of institutional autonomy. This description matches a small fraction of the total number of libraries; happily, the monthly review cycle can be adapted to work in a variety of libraries. Some ideas follow for developing processes that may work in smaller libraries, libraries with flat staffing structures, and libraries that exist within larger institutional structures.

Variations for Library Size

A smaller library led by a library director and staffed by a few full- and part-time staff members may adapt the monthly review cycle in several ways. Operational area meetings could be replaced with one-on-one or small group meetings between the library director and the staff in each area. In this scenario, the library director does the work of the planning team on their own, communicating and collaborating on the plan with staff during these meetings. Formal reports from each operational area are less important as the library director would be collecting this information to add directly to the monthly library review report. This adaptation works best in libraries with a staff configuration that aligns closely to the operational areas.

Another possibility for smaller libraries is for the library director to hold a monthly staff meeting that combines the functions of the operational area meetings and the planning team meeting. During the monthly staff meeting, staff are asked to share progress on action plans and observations on information behavior and emerging information needs. The library director shares a preliminary draft of the monthly review report for discussion and input from the staff. After the meeting, the library director then completes the monthly review report and distributes it to the staff. Assessment and tracking between the monthly staff meetings is the responsibility of the library director, who checks in with staff on an as-needed basis. This adaptation works better for libraries whose staff members overlap and cooperate on action plans in more than one operational area.

It is possible to scale the monthly review cycle down even further for use by solo librarians. The solo librarian handles the work of the entire library without the assistance of other professional librarians. In some cases, the solo librarian may have assistance from paraprofessionals or volunteers. The solo librarian can carry out most of the monthly review cycle independently, though it becomes even more important to make sure whatever process is developed meets the three objectives. Each objective poses different challenges in a solo librarian setting. At the very least the solo librarian may discover the need for a conversation partner to assist with the assessment and planning pieces. This person could be a paraprofessional or dedicated volunteer working in the library. In some cases, it might also be helpful to consider partnering with a fellow solo librarian who is also implementing an integrated plan. Such a partnership could help with objectivity and accountability.

Variations for Staffing Models

For libraries with staffing models and structures that are less hierarchical, there are ways to customize the monthly review cycle process to preserve an egalitarian ethos. A library that lacks firm departmental divisions and has a library director who supervises the entire staff represents a flat staffing model. The staff may consist of several full-time members, some of whom may be professional librarians. In this type of setting, the library director may organize the staff into teams by organizational area. Another option is to allow staff to self-organize into teams based on the action plans they are working on and the organizational area most closely aligned with their responsibilities in each month. Staff might take turns leading the organizational area meetings and participating in the planning team. Rotating this responsibility among different staff members contributes to staff development and provides opportunity for new and fresh perspectives on the planning team as the plan develops and matures.

These adaptations to the monthly review cycle highlight the fluid nature of a flat staffing model. The library director is responsible for maintaining the broad, big-picture view of the entire integrated plan. As the responsibility for leading organizational area meetings rotates among the staff, consistent record keeping and reporting for each organizational area becomes important, preventing the loss of important insights and follow-ups during leadership transitions. Communication between and among staff becomes crucial for easy and seamless transitions.

Variations for Institutional Structure

The monthly review cycle takes on a slightly different shape when implemented in libraries whose administrative structure is intertwined with a larger institution. This may include libraries embedded in larger institutions, such as academic libraries or corporate libraries. It could also include libraries that are part of a branch library system or consortium. Such libraries may have to plan within tighter constraints or obtain additional approval before making changes to goals, outcomes, and action plans. The monthly review report becomes an incredibly important tool for communicating to higher-level administration what is happening in the library. When adjustments are needed, these reports provide relevant facts, making it easier for the library to propose changes. In the best cases, higher-level administration is not surprised by requests for adjustment because the monthly review reports have clearly articulated the process of discovering and investigating emerging needs or challenges related to action plans.

Likewise, these types of libraries may receive requests from higher-level administration informing and influencing the integrated plan. Requests could include mandates to pursue a particular project or explore a new avenue for library services. While the need may not have emerged from the assessment and evaluation process built into the library's integrated plan and monthly review cycle, these requests can be handled similarly to the collected observations of patron information behavior. They can be recorded in the monthly review report, incorporated into the goals and strategic outcomes, broken down into action plans, and scheduled on the rolling horizon—taking into consideration any deadlines imposed and adjusting existing action plans accordingly to maintain balance across operational areas and staff workload.

In these situations, communication shifts from two-way to three-way by incorporating the external administrative structure as much as is reasonable. The library director or the planning team runs the risk of being put in the middle of library staff and higher-level administration, so careful attention needs to be given to keeping conversation consistent and open among all parties. Animosity can grow when information is not shared in a timely manner, resulting in a group feeling blindsided or ignored. Transparency, excellent documentation, and a commitment to open communication by everyone is extremely important to the success of the monthly review cycle in this type of library.

Summary

With the preparation and organizational work complete, this chapter covered the process of implementing a library's integrated plan through a monthly review cycle. The monthly review cycle is a routine established and overseen by library leadership, keeping the integrated plan moving forward. It has three objectives: to facilitate communication among library staff about what is going on within and around the library, to routinize assessment practices so that they foster a sense of curiosity about the library's operations, and to perpetually plan forward on the rolling horizon. There are several activities that library staff participate in during the monthly review cycle. These include making assessments of the library's operation in relation to the goals and strategic outcomes in the integrated plan, reconciling the library's finances, and collecting and analyzing data on information needs and behavior.

Much of the activity of the monthly review cycle takes place either in meetings, in preparation for meetings, or in a follow-up to a meeting. Keeping the three objectives of the monthly review cycle at the forefront ensures that implementation is smooth, and the integrated plan is successful. Be mindful to promote good communication among library staff, particularly in relation to the integrated plan. Invest time in developing strong and healthy communication practices that promote good conversation, honor boundaries, and build trust. When assessing library operations, ask good questions and try to remain impartial and objective. Utilize both quantitative and qualitative methods for collecting data about the library's operations. Strive for balance and efficiency when scheduling plans on the rolling horizon. Utilize visual tools, such as a Gantt chart, to track actions and staff workload.

The product of the monthly review cycle is a monthly review report. Much of what is shared and discussed during the monthly review cycle is recorded in the report. The report has four main components: assessments of progress toward strategic outcomes and goals, a financial summary, information needs and behavior analysis, and updates to the integrated plan. These components can be organized, ordered, and presented in a way that is most helpful and appropriate for the library. The assessment sections can be as simple as a bulleted list of completed actions and updates or as complex as a dashboard with graphs and charts. The financial summary helps reconcile expenditures and receipts monthly while tracking whether spending is on budget and income is as projected. There is space to record and report quantitative and qualitative data, including observations gleaned from information behavior research. Analysis of these data and observations becomes part of the monthly review narrative, bringing to light possible new trends that may be considered when adjusting the integrated plan. The report also serves as a record of how the components of the integrated plan change over time. Revisions to strategic outcomes and goals, and at times updates to mission and vision statements, are included in the report with updates to the planning charts.

A library does not need to be middle- to large-sized with a hierarchical staffing model and a fair amount of autonomy to implement the monthly review cycle and an integrated plan. The cycle is customizable and adaptable to suit libraries of various sizes, staffing models, and institutional structures. Several examples and suggestions are given for smaller libraries, libraries with solo librarians, libraries with flat or egalitarian staffing models, and libraries that are embedded within larger organizations. There are many ways to structure the monthly review cycle and organize the monthly review report. If the core objectives are reached and all the key pieces of information are explored and presented, your monthly review cycle and monthly review report will keep the library's integrated plan moving forward.

Preliminary: Pivoting toward an integrated future
Stage 1: Foundation and groundwork
Stage 2. Building a planning structure
Stage 3. Implementing a monthly review cycle
➡ Stage 4. Long-term assessment and adjustment

CHAPTER 6

Long-Term Assessment and Adjustment

Once your library's integrated plan is in place and a monthly review cycle is implemented, it may seem that the work is complete. The plan can run itself from this point as the library administrator sits back and watches it unfold, right? Wrong. Integrated Library Planning requires attention, care, and thought to be sustained for the long term. In many ways, the true work begins here, when the library begins living into the plan. The monthly review cycle is designed to help library staff and administrators accomplish the tasks included in the plan as well as to continually explore opportunities to revise the plan. Each month, the integrated plan continues to grow and strengthen. It adapts to the library's rhythms and challenges staff and administration to look at the plan critically and strategically as it is carried out.

Unlike the development and implementation of a library's integrated plan, long-term assessment and adjustment does not have a set of clear steps and actions. There are certainly things one may expect to encounter, but the way each library's integrated plan unfolds is unique to the library creating and maintaining it. Therefore, it becomes important to hone the skills and practices learned during the development and implementation of the plan. As the plan shifts into this long-term phase, these skills and practices are what make or break the ongoing assessment and adjustment of the plan as it matures.

While this chapter contains some wisdom and advice on how to live into the monthly review cycle and adjust the integrated plan, it is most important to remember this: once Integrated Library Planning and the monthly review cycle are implemented, they become a dynamic part of your library. Much like tending a garden or caring for a pet, the integrated plan gives back what you put into it. If one element of the plan is not achieving the expected results, it is not a reason to scrap the entire plan and start over. Rather it is an invitation to look deeper, analyze further, and think more creatively about the plan. The integrated plan is more than a roadmap to achieve goals and strategic outcomes; it is an opportunity to imagine new solutions.

This chapter covers many aspects of living into Integrated Library Planning that a library administrator may expect:

- responding to observed information behavior strategically;
- allowing monthly financial review to inform and impact decision making;
- adding new action plans while navigating a rolling horizon effectively;
- revising goals and strategic outcomes over time; and,
- integrating assessment and review cycles a library may be subjected to from institutional or external authorities.

This is not a definitive list of everything a library may expect to encounter as the integrated plan matures. These are just a few of the major challenges that arise as a library lives into its integrated plan.

Strategically Responding to Observed Information Behavior

Observing information behavior and identifying emerging information needs are key practices as the library engages with the monthly review cycle. The integrated plan stays relevant as observations recorded in the monthly review report are converted into actionable elements. Care must be taken, however, to avoid acting on observations too quickly. The objective is to respond strategically, not to react recklessly.

A strategic response to observed information behavior begins with further research. As mentioned in the previous chapter, deeper research into and analysis of observed information behavior is part of the monthly review cycle. Observations are shared and recorded in the monthly library review report. Those that spark additional research are tracked from month to month until an emerging information need is identified. Additional research may come in the form of gathering quantitative statistical data, qualitative research using surveys or interviews, or a mixture of these methods.

Once an emerging information need is identified, before deciding whether to address the need, it is important to evaluate it in light of the library's mission and vision. Does it fit within the purview of the library as it presently understands itself? It is crucial to understand your library's place within its connected communities. Information needs perceived and identified in your patron's use of the library may or may not be a reflection on something you as the library administrator have control over. Sometimes an information need arises from conditions external to the library. Depending on the need, it may present an opportunity to influence change in a wider sphere through raising awareness and activism, if such activities fall within the library's mission and vision. If addressing the identified emerging information need clearly falls within the library's mission and vision, then proceed with incorporating it into the integrated plan. Otherwise, the library cannot and should not attempt to address the need.

To incorporate an emerging information need into the integrated plan, it must be assigned to a goal and strategic outcome within an operational area and broken down into action plans. It does not necessarily matter which of these parts comes first. For some, it may make more sense to start with operational area as the broadest level and work inward toward defining specific action plans. For others, it may be easier to create the action plans first and then find the operational area, goal, and strategic outcome best suited to house the plans. This does not have to be a strict linear process and can accommodate fluid, organic development. Regardless of the order in which it is completed, all the key elements of the integrated plan need to be addressed for the emerging information need to be ready for full incorporation into the plan.

When thinking about the most appropriate place to incorporate the emerging information need into the integrated plan, look at the whole system of operational areas and divisions, goals, and strategic outcomes that exist in the plan. Is there a combination of area/goal/outcome that is a good match for the new action plans being introduced to the plan? If so, the task of finding a place for the emerging need in your plan is easy and straightforward. There are times, however, when one of these elements is appropriate, but others do not fit well with the emerging need. In these cases, do not be discouraged. This is one of several moments in Integrated Library Planning when things can be changed and updated to accommodate new additions to the plan. Types of changes and updates include adding a new goal or strategic outcome, adjusting an existing goal or outcome, and reorganizing divisions or operational areas along with their respective goals and outcomes.

98   Chapter 6

Any of these changes to the plan to accommodate an emerging information need will have an impact on existing action plans. Therefore, when considering how to incorporate an emerging information need into the integrated plan, look at the existing action plans. Are there any that overlap or directly conflict with the new action plans being generated to address the emerging need? How will changing a particular goal or strategic outcome impact the existing plans already under it? Strategically responding to observed information behavior and incorporating an emerging information need includes consideration of existing action plans. Careful evaluation of action plans and how they are impacted by the changes to the plan is important. Existing action plans with competing objectives may need to be reevaluated, depending on the priority of the emerging information need. If goals and strategic outcomes change during the process of incorporating an emerging information need, the changes should be inclusive of the existing action plans if those action plans are to remain in effect after the plan is revised.

Depending on the scope of the emerging information need, it may make sense to create one or more new action plans. The action plans are the pathway toward meeting both the emerging need as well as the library's goals and strategic outcomes. The process of creating action plans at this point in the life of the integrated plan is much the same as creating them during the second phase. Break the work of addressing the emerging information need into actionable tasks that can be tracked and measured. These should be manageable tasks, clearly defined and able to be scheduled. In the process of creating the action plans, think about how the plans will be accomplished and who will be responsible for them. How will you assess and track them when they are underway? When will you know they have been completed? Before the action plans are finalized, review their placement in the integrated plan to ensure that no further adjustments are needed to the operating area, goal, and strategic outcome where they are housed.

Once the action plans are set, they must be scheduled and incorporated into the rolling planning horizon. Consider the new action plans and their relationship to existing plans already mapped onto the rolling horizon. What is their priority? Are they dependent upon the completion of action plans already scheduled? Is there an optimal time of year to pursue these new action plans? All of these factors must be considered when determining where to place the new action plans on the rolling horizon. While scheduling them at the end of the planning horizon, where there is more space in the schedule, may seem the easiest and most straightforward path, that may not be optimal for the new action plans or for the integrated plan as a whole. One of the key objectives of Integrated Library Planning is to be able to respond to emerging needs in a timely manner. Recall the research that supported incorporating the emerging information need into the integrated plan and the factors driving the need. This information, combined with a full understanding of the library's rhythms and how the new action plans will interact with existing action plans, is crucial for optimal scheduling. Once scheduled, the transformation of the emerging information need into actionable plans incorporated into the integrated plan is complete.

Case Study

Phone calls are regularly tracked as part of the Ruffin Library's reference desk statistics. While conducting monthly analysis of the reference log, library staff notice repeated questions received by phone. Most of the questions, such as when is the library open and what is its policy on material donations, can be answered by visiting Ruffin Library's website. The number of phone calls received add up to a considerable amount of staff time spent answering calls or returning voicemail messages.

Over the span of three months, it becomes clear that the number of basic questions the library receives by phone is steady. Although the information is readily available on the library's website, callers are either not able to access the internet or not able to locate the information on the library's website. This prompts additional investigation into Ruffin Library's website and the nature of the calls. How easy is it to navigate the library's website? How many clicks does it take to find answers to the most frequently asked questions? Who are the library's most frequent callers?

Targeted research into these questions reveals some interesting insights. First, Ruffin Library's most frequent callers are patrons from the surrounding community. They are not students, faculty, or staff, who would be accustomed to first looking online for information about the library. Second, some of the questions are answered by information found easily on the library's main homepage while other questions have answers buried on the library policies webpage. One solution is to add to a Frequently Asked Questions database with information for phone callers, but that would likely not have an impact on the observed behavior that callers do not turn to an internet search or the library's website for answers first.

Brainstorming with staff who answer these calls leads to an idea to add an automated menu to the circulation desk phone. Callers would immediately be routed to a recording with options to select based on the type of their inquiry. Prerecorded messages for each option would provide basic information as well as an option to be forwarded to a staff member for further information. This idea turns into an action plan: "Review telephone set up and explore possibility of adding menus to direct callers." This action plan is further divided into individual actions or steps and assigned to staff members. In reviewing the integrated plan, this action plan fits nicely under an existing strategic outcome in the Services operational area: "Patrons are able to ask questions and get timely responses from wherever they are with whatever communication technology they have available." The scheduling of this action plan is coordinated with staff workloads and placed on the library's rolling planning horizon.

Within seven months of the initial observation, Ruffin Library successfully implements an automated menu with several prerecorded answers to the most asked questions. Patrons now no longer need to wait for a staff member to answer the phone or return their call to find out when the library is open or how to drop off a donation. Most callers get the information they need quickly, and staff spend less time returning phone calls. The result directly contributes to the Ruffin Library's strategic outcome that patrons using telephones can ask questions and receive timely responses.

Incorporating Financial Review into Decision Making

As one of the main components of the monthly review cycle, financial review can be incorporated into decisions as a library's integrated plan progresses. Many action plans have a financial impact on the library; few are cost neutral. As action plans are added to the plan and scheduled onto the rolling planning horizon, the financial review is an important consideration in the decision-making process.

The financial review primarily helps track spending in relation to the integrated plan. Through the process of reconciling the library's finances each month, the monthly review report may include a summary of expenditures and income as well as a snapshot of the library's budget. This snapshot shows the health of the library's budget, identifying which accounts still have funds remaining, which are nearly depleted, and which are overdrawn. This is a helpful reference for administrators, who can see if funds are currently available in the budget when an emerging need leads to the development of new action plans. The practice of financial review as part of Integrated Library Planning makes it possible to move forward with new action plans efficiently when funds exist in the budget to support them.

For new action plans with costs that exceed the current fiscal year's budget, additional planning is needed. Are funds available in the next fiscal year's budget? Or does the plan require funds outside of what is normally included in the budget? If funds are available in the next fiscal year's budget, then adding the action plan to the rolling horizon involves scheduling it at a time when those funds will be available. If the new action plan requires funds beyond the planned budget, then there are two possible courses of action. The first would be to identify additional sources of funding for the action plan. These sources may come from fundraising or from a special grant, for example. If additional activities, such as special events or grant writing, are needed to raise funds for an action plan, then these activities must also be scheduled and tracked on the rolling horizon.

The second possible course of action to secure funding for new action plans would be to create a budget proposal for the new fiscal year. For most library administrators, proposing a budget for the new fiscal year is part of the rhythm of library business. When creating the budget proposal, consult the rolling horizon to anticipate the costs of action plans in the new fiscal year. Analyze spending in the current fiscal year. Look for opportunities to reallocate funds in the new fiscal year to align more closely with the priorities of the integrated plan. Build a budget proposal that draws on this analysis and adequately funds the projected expenditures of future action plans. When presenting the budget proposal, the integrated plan provides support and documentation for the library's budget requests to reallocate or increase funding.

Estimating costs is an important aspect of financial review as it informs and impacts the integrated plan. Sometimes estimating costs is a simple process. When an action plan is straightforward and estimates received from vendors and service providers are accurate, the proposed budget can easily accommodate spending. There are occasions, however, when estimated costs are lower than actual costs. In these cases, the integrated plan can help administrators identify how to best cover these additional costs. Sometimes it is possible to divert funding from other action plans. This may or may not involve rescheduling action plans to free up funds from other places in the budget. At other times, the integrated plan may reveal other possibilities, such as coordinating additional funding for an action plan with other action plans also in process.

Every so often, the library administrator is presented with the happiness of a budget surplus toward the end of the fiscal year. Budget surpluses occur when actual costs are lower than anticipated costs or when action plans are canceled or postponed until a future fiscal year. There are usually many deals available to library administrators at the end of the fiscal year as vendors are trying to boost their sales before closing out the year. Knowing which ones would be a good investment for the library comes from the integrated plan. When presented with a budget surplus, all the elements of the monthly review cycle inform decision making, resulting in wise end-of-year spending.

Case Study

The King Memorial Library has a self-checkout kiosk for patrons to use when library staff are occupied assisting other patrons. The kiosk does not have a keyboard or a touch screen, only a barcode scanner. For patrons to log into their library accounts and check out books, they must first scan their library card. However, patrons have become accustomed to not needing their library cards. King Memorial Library is a small community public library. Library staff often recognize repeat patrons and look up accounts by a simple name search. For patrons who are not frequent visitors, library staff will accept a photo ID in lieu of a library card. With the new self-checkout kiosk in place, library staff are observing that it gets little use as patrons are not in the habit of carrying their library cards with them.

One possible solution for greater access to the self-checkout kiosk is for the library to offer electronic library cards accessible on smartphones or mobile devices. If a patron had a mobile device with them—and most King Memorial Library patrons do—the patron could access the electronic version of their library card and use that to log into the self-checkout kiosk. King Memorial Library reaches out to the support company that handles their open-source library system. Is it possible to provide an electronic library card that patrons can view from their account information page? The developers at the support company assure the library that yes, it is possible but requires a small development fee. This solution potentially benefits many libraries. Once the development is complete, the electronic library card feature will become part of the next release and all libraries using this open-source library system will have access to this new feature.

When the library receives the estimate for the development of an electronic library card, it does not take long to decide. King Memorial Library's financial review and projections show that there will be a small budget surplus sufficient to cover the development fee. Looking ahead to the next fiscal year, the library will be losing a few part-time staff hours due to budget cuts, affecting the number of staff at the circulation desk. The need for easier access to the self-checkout kiosk will only become deeper as circulation desk staffing decreases. Understanding the priority of the need and seeing that the cost can be absorbed into the budget, the library funds the open-source development project. The development timeline is added into the integrated plan, providing space for library staff to help test, implement, train, and promote the new electronic library card feature. Informed by a goal to provide greater access to information, King Memorial Library's funding of this open-source project addressed an emerging need in their community while also benefitting similar libraries and communities using the same open-source library system. Making an informed and timely decision based on their integrated plan, this library is also expanding their impact through investment in the worldwide open-source library community.

The Rolling Horizon and Adding New Action Plans

Once Integrated Library Planning is implemented and the monthly review process has begun, your library buzzes with orchestrated activity. Action plans are being completed and new action plans are being added. All this activity affects the rolling horizon. Once implemented the rolling horizon becomes one of the most dynamic elements of the integrated plan. There are multiple layers of movement on the rolling horizon. One is the passage of time that keeps the horizon perpetually moving forward one month at a time. Another layer of movement is the positioning and repositioning of action plans on the horizon as external and internal forces cause changes and shifts. Yet another layer is the appearance and disappearance of action plans from the rolling horizon because of assessing and considering emerging needs. Working with a rolling horizon is far more complex than simply tacking a new month to the end and filling it with new action plans. Actively maintaining a rolling horizon involves ongoing consideration, planning, and critical evaluation to maximize effectiveness.

The rolling horizon is reviewed and rolled forward as part of the monthly review cycle. Rather than keeping everything in its place and viewing the newest month at the end of the horizon as a blank canvas, it is most helpful to consider the entire period of the rolling horizon as a blank canvas. A review of the action plans mapped to the horizon needs to include these questions:

- What priority level does an action plan have?
- When is the appropriate timing for a particular action plan?
- Is the time to complete an action plan estimated correctly?

- Is this action plan dependent upon the completion of any other action plans?
- How will working on this action plan affect overall staff workload?
- Can an action plan be grouped with similar action plans scheduled near the same time to maximize efficiency?

Many of these questions were considered during the second phase of the Integrated Library Planning process when the starter action plans were first mapped onto the rolling horizon. It is critical to keep them in mind during the monthly review cycle so that adjustments to the rolling horizon are in keeping with the library's goals and strategic outcomes.

Ask the same questions to schedule a new action plan on the rolling horizon. If this is a higher priority action plan, it will likely need to be scheduled at the earliest possible time in the rolling horizon. If it is time-sensitive and can only be completed at a particular time in the year, that will also affect when it is scheduled. If it is similar to action plans already mapped onto the horizon, there may be an opportunity to schedule the new one with them. It is also possible that a new action plan may replace the need for an action plan that is already scheduled. In these cases, the older action plan may be replaced or substituted with the newer one. These factors represent the many considerations that are weighed when scheduling new action plans onto the rolling horizon.

Once new action plans are added to the rolling horizon, the entire horizon needs to be checked for workload balance. The goal is to schedule action plans across the rolling horizon so that everyone on staff can expect a consistent level of work confluent with the library's rhythms. For example, if a library has fewer patrons visiting the library during the summer months and less staff time is spent on reference and circulation services during that time, it may be appropriate to schedule additional action plans for completion that would engage these staff members during this time. Libraries with staff working across multiple divisions and areas of operations also need to look at workload balance for individual staff members. It is quite possible for the rolling horizon to look balanced within an area or across multiple areas within a division while the staff members assigned to those action plans may have multiple deadlines in one month and none the next. Vacations, holidays, and extended closures are also important to factor into the rolling horizon because they impact the amount of time available within a month to work on action plans.

Even with the most careful and attentive planning process, it is possible for action plans to fall behind schedule resulting in missed deadlines and delays to dependent action plans. Life happens, including unexpected complications or external delays that could not have been anticipated during planning. Sometimes, it may just take longer than expected to complete a project. Estimating the amount of time to complete an action plan is a skill developed and strengthened over time as the integrated plan matures and as the library administrator gains experience. There are many factors impacting the amount of time an action plan takes to complete: the scope of the project, the physical capacity needed to complete the project, and the skill and productivity rate of the staff assigned to the project. The environment may also play an important role. For example, staff whose workstations are in a public area are more likely to be interrupted during a task than those whose workstations are in a restricted staff area. Frequent interruptions can prolong the amount of time it takes to complete a task.

When action plans fall behind, adjustments must be made across the entire rolling horizon to ensure that the success and continuation of the integrated plan is not put at risk. A measured approach is helpful. At the close of the month, mark action plans that were scheduled to be completed but are not. These can go on a watch list or marked as needing attention in the monthly review report. Seek feedback from the staff working on the action plans to see how far behind schedule they are and how much time they estimate needing to complete the project. For plans that will be completed within the next month with little to no impact on future action plans, no adjustments may be needed. The next month's review report will show that they were completed slightly behind schedule. For action plans severely behind schedule, usually because of unforeseen complications or competing priorities with other action plans in process, a more careful assessment of the situation is needed. Should work on an action plan be suspended until a later date on the rolling horizon? Or should the deadline be extended and future action plans be rescheduled to accommodate the extension? The better choice likely depends upon timing, availability, and workload balance. Library administrators make more effective decisions in these situations when there is time to step back and take in the entire landscape of the integrated plan.

Case Study

The technical services department at Lewis College Library has a goal for optimal discoverability of materials in the library's collections. One strategic outcome is to ensure that linked data in the catalog is in excellent condition. An action plan scheduled on the library's rolling horizon is to clean up the records in their authority file. The two staff members in the technical services department estimate it will take twenty months to complete a review and cleanup of the 200,000 authority records in the library's catalog system.

As they begin their work, they notice that some authority records are not attached to bibliographic records. This is because another action plan is being carried out concurrently to rightsize the collection by deselecting materials that are out of scope. As bibliographic records for deselected materials are removed, they leave behind orphan authority records. While these orphaned authority records will eventually be removed by an automatic process, it is wasteful of staff time and a drain on morale to clean up authority records scheduled for deletion through the deaccessioning project.

This problem is brought up during the next technical services area review and passed on to the administrative team that compiles the monthly review report. When the administrative team looks at the rolling horizon, they see that the deaccessioning project is scheduled to be complete in five months. While the strategic outcome that the authority file cleanup addresses is critically important, the administrative team agrees that it can be put on hold until the deaccessioning project is complete.

Because the two technical services staff are no longer working on the authority file cleanup, they have additional time to spend assisting with the deaccessioning project. As a result, that action plan is completed within four months instead of five. When the technical services staff resume their work on authority records, they find that there are now only 160,000 authority records in the Lewis College Library's catalog. They estimate it will take just sixteen months to complete the project, placing the projected completion at the same point on the rolling horizon as it was originally. This time, however, the technical services staff have the assurance that their work will remain a valuable part of the library's catalog and not rendered obsolete when already cleaned authority records are orphaned by a deaccessioning project.

Revising Goals and Strategic Outcomes

One of the distinctive characteristics of Integrated Library Planning is that the monthly review cycle keeps the library's goals and strategic outcomes in the forefront. These are not lofty and ephemeral objectives that sit on a shelf to be admired. These are active aspirations subject to timely revision as a library's environment and patrons change. As part of the monthly review cycle, consideration of goals and strategic outcomes is critical to keeping the entire integrated plan relevant and responsive.

A natural time to revise goals and strategic outcomes is when all the action plans under a strategic outcome are complete. This is an opportunity to ask if the library has now reached that strategic outcome. In theory, once all the action plans are complete the library can say it has achieved the strategic outcome; removing the strategic outcome from the plan or replacing it is an easy course of action. In actuality, the resolution of the outcome and next steps are rarely this clear. Sometimes additional action plans are needed to further the progress toward the strategic outcome. In these cases, keep the strategic outcome as part of the integrated plan and simply add new action plans to map onto the rolling horizon. At other times, the outcome originally identified may be deemed insufficient or ill-fitting in retrospect. On these occasions, revise the strategic outcome, add new action plans, and map them onto the rolling horizon.

A strategic outcome does not have to be bereft of active action plans to be reconsidered. Even when new action plans are added to existing strategic outcomes, they can develop and shift over time. Attention should be given to how well the strategic outcome connects to its parent goal. While the goal is most often written as a "to" statement, a strategic outcome should be stated as if the goal is realized. If a direct connection cannot be made between the goal and the strategic outcome, then one or the other needs to be revised until that connection is clear. When revising a goal to better suit a particular strategic outcome, the other strategic outcomes connected to that goal need to be reviewed as well. Goals, strategic outcomes, and action plans are a complex puzzle of interconnected pieces. When one shifts, it can cause inconsistencies elsewhere. This is both a tremendous strength and challenge in Integrated Library Planning. It requires nimbleness to be able to change perspectives, zoom in and out frequently, and look at library operations from all angles to make sure that everything in the plan remains aligned.

All libraries have actions or tasks that repeat at some frequency. For the rolling planning horizon to function as an accurate estimator of staff workload, it is helpful to represent these repeating and ongoing tasks as action plans. There are several ways to do this. One is to establish strategic outcomes specifically for repeating or cyclical action plans. This allows you to continue ongoing tasks under the same strategic outcome, though it will be difficult to show progress toward that strategic outcome. Another option is to create strategic outcomes tied to a unit of time, like an academic year or a fiscal year. Embedding ongoing tasks and repeating action plans within a strategic outcome tied to a specific unit of time, allows administrators to acknowledge when an outcome is achieved and affords the opportunity to revise the outcome before it is reused for the next iteration of the cycle (see figure 17).

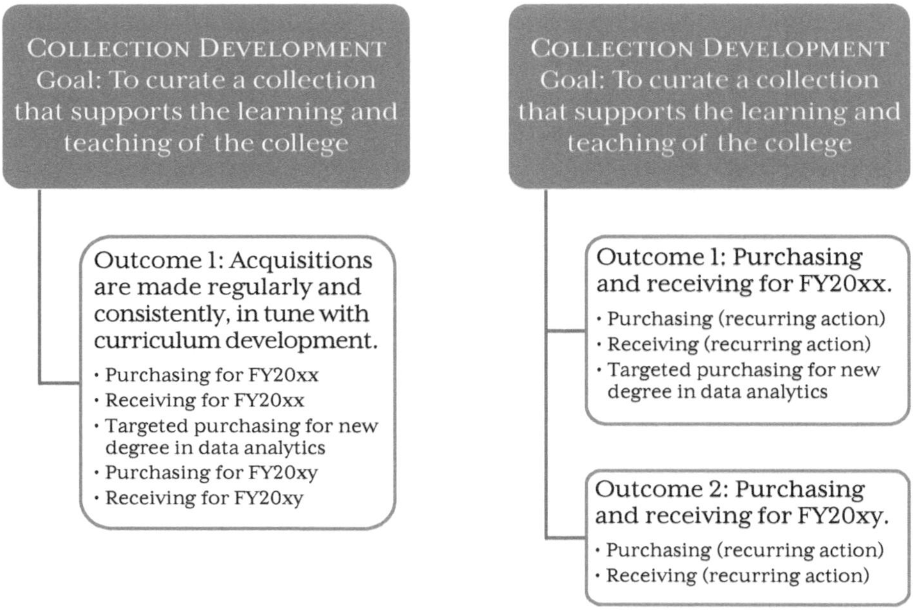

COLLECTION DEVELOPMENT
Goal: To curate a collection that supports the learning and teaching of the college

Outcome 1: Acquisitions are made regularly and consistently, in tune with curriculum development.
- Purchasing for FY20xx
- Receiving for FY20xx
- Targeted purchasing for new degree in data analytics
- Purchasing for FY20xy
- Receiving for FY20xy

COLLECTION DEVELOPMENT
Goal: To curate a collection that supports the learning and teaching of the college

Outcome 1: Purchasing and receiving for FY20xx.
- Purchasing (recurring action)
- Receiving (recurring action)
- Targeted purchasing for new degree in data analytics

Outcome 2: Purchasing and receiving for FY20xy.
- Purchasing (recurring action)
- Receiving (recurring action)

FIGURE 17

Two examples of incorporating repeating actions into goals and outcomes within a library's integrated plan. The example on the left shows an outcome that is not tied to a length of time. The action plans connected to the outcome are for repeating actions that take place across a fiscal year. As time progresses, action plans will be completed but the outcome will remain. The example on the right shows outcomes that are tied to a fiscal year. Recurring actions are connected to these outcomes. There is also the ability to add new actions specific to the outcome's fiscal year period. At the end of the fiscal year, the outcome will be complete and can be reported as such in an annual summary report. Furthermore, reflection on the work toward the outcome can inform any changes or revisions to the outcome established for future fiscal year periods.

Revisiting goals and strategic outcomes is also necessary when there are shifts in workflow and process in the library. These shifts may have internal or external forces behind them. They could be caused by anything from a change in staffing to a change in institutional expectations. Arguably, such shifts are inevitable if the library's integrated plan is effective in dynamically responding to changing needs and emerging trends. When this happens simply revising goals or adding new strategic outcomes may not fit the need. Goals might need to be looked at within the context of all goals in the plan. Are there any that might be combined? This level of review could also extend to the way in which the library's operations are organized. Particularly in situations that involve a change in staffing, the library's divisions and areas of operations might need to be redefined along with their corresponding goals.

This level of change and revision in an integrated plan need not be daunting or frightening. Extreme change might be expected every three to five years on a traditional strategic planning cycle, but an integrated plan gives library administrators the freedom to incorporate change and revision whenever it is most needed. While some stability is appreciated by library staff members—a case for not making these types of changes frequently—there is a tremendous amount of power and flexibility in being able to tweak high levels of the integrated plan when it is most needed. It makes the difference between a timely response to an emerging need and a frustrated acknowledgement of need for change with no space or mechanism available to make it happen.

Case Study

Tubman Library's integrated plan starts out with separate operational areas, each with corresponding goals and outcomes for communications, exhibits, and fundraising. Several months into the plan, the library staff notes the interrelated nature of these three operational areas. Fundraising depends almost entirely on communication: promoting library events, raising awareness of ways to support the library, and maintaining correspondence with important donors. Exhibits, which includes the library's displays, provides opportunities to connect with donors and likewise includes various marketing and communications campaigns. Communication encompasses promotion of all library events and activities, potentially impacting fundraising, though that purpose is not included in the goal.

Working with the plan over a period of six months, staff notice significant overlap among these areas as well as some gaps in the goals for each. As long as these three operational areas are considered separate, there is little opportunity to envision outreach strategies more broadly. To continue moving the library forward, the library staff needs to examine ways to bring attention to the library's events and activities as well as to its collections and services, while also strengthening a donor base and raising money for special projects and exhibits. Doing so would also ensure that library staff time and resources are being used efficiently and effectively.

During the monthly review cycle, Tubman Library's director and department heads collaborate on a change to the integrated plan's organizational structure. The three areas in question—communications, exhibits, and fundraising—are combined into one area called outreach. The goals for each of these areas are initially merged as goals for the new outreach area, offering a regular opportunity to recognize the interrelated nature of communication, promotion of the library's collection through exhibits, and raising funds for library collections and services. Because of the monthly review cycle, Tubman Library is able to make this change efficiently and in a timely manner. Combining the three areas into one also results in new ways of thinking about how the library approaches outreach. Over time, the library director begins to see that outreach is one of the most under-resourced areas of the library as well as an area with tremendous potential for positive impact on the library's growth. Diligent work through the monthly review cycle reveals this untapped potential and backs it with solid statistics and assessment. When an opportunity opens to hire a new staff person at the library, the search committee crafts a position with greater emphasis on outreach, furthering the library's progress toward its goals and vision.

Integrating External Review Cycles

A library does not operate in a vacuum. Academic libraries are embedded in institutions of higher education, public libraries relate to municipal governments, and special libraries are extensions of the organizations they serve, such as law firms and healthcare facilities. Therefore, library administrators must always be prepared to report on library activities to institutional leaders outside of the library and adapt to whatever change may be implemented on an institutional level. Many parent institutions have their own strategic plans and review cycles. An integrated plan with a monthly review cycle is flexible and able to accommodate and integrate these external review cycles. External review cycles include institutional strategic planning, reporting to and conducting self-assessments for accrediting bodies, and other reviews initiated at the higher levels of the library's parent organization.

The integrated plan and monthly review cycle can inform and be informed by external review cycles. It is a two-way flow of information and influence (see figure 18). On one side, Integrated Library Planning and the monthly review cycle produces data, observations, and findings helpful in an external review. External review cycles are usually data-hungry processes. While the monthly review may not include every type of quantitative and qualitative data needed for the external review, it is likely that much of the information in the monthly review will be helpful and may be reused. On the other side, the external review cycle can influence how the integrated plan is structured, what questions are

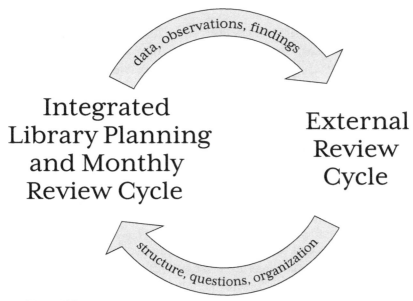

FIGURE 18
How Integrated Library Planning and a monthly review cycle informs and is informed by an external review cycle.

asked, and how data is organized for the monthly review. This is particularly the case for external review cycles that repeat without much change to their process. For example, an accrediting body may ask for the same types of data every fiscal year. Those report questions can be incorporated into the integrated plan and monthly review. This serves two purposes. First, it helps structure and organize the data collected for the monthly review in a way that is easily reusable for external review. Second, it extends reflection on the data collected for external review into the monthly review cycle, creating additional space to assess and pivot as changes occur and needs emerge.

There is one major caveat to this two-way flow of information and influence between the integrated plan and an external review cycle. When integrating structure, questions, and organization alongside sharing data, observations, and findings, it is critically important to remain open during the evaluation, analysis, and assessment that occurs during both the monthly review cycle and the external review cycle. Integrating external review cycles into the monthly review cycle can be a tremendous time-saver and source of efficiency, but it should not be a shortcut. The monthly review cycle is appropriately distinct from an external review cycle. Each will have its own objectives, offering an opportunity to

112   Chapter 6

view the library's operations from different perspectives. Optimally, an external review cycle offers new insights and perspectives that can then be used to adjust the integrated plan. Reusing and reappropriating the monthly review report for an external review cycle without taking the time reassess and reevaluate the information being presented for external review is a tragic missed opportunity.

Case Study

Marshall University is seeking reaccreditation as a degree-granting institution of higher education. It offers both undergraduate and graduate programs. The Marshall University Library supports the university's degree programs and maintains special collections and archives of interest to researchers. As part of its reaccreditation, Marshall University conducts a self-study of its mission and institutional priorities and how well they meet the standards of the accrediting body. One of the standards relates to library access and services, so the library director is called upon to provide information for the self-study report.

The Marshall University Library has used an integrated plan for the past three years, but the period for the self-study report is eight years. The library director can draw upon three years of monthly review reports plus the initial planning documents generated to create the integrated plan. This streamlines data collection and collation, though additional research is required to report on the first five years of the eight-year self-study period. Also, in anticipation of the self-study, the library director already went through the process of connecting the components of the accreditor's standard relating to library access and services to the goals of the library's integrated plan. Drafting the library portion of the self-study report goes smoothly since so much planning work had been completed in advance. The library director has all the necessary data for the report. The library director is also able to articulate clearly how the library has met the standards established by the accrediting body by including narratives from the monthly review reports relating to progress toward goals that align with the standards.

Once all the information is collected for the self-study report, the library director participates in a series of conversations to go over the findings. While the library director can easily connect data related to library access and services to the accreditation standards, these conversations reveal new insights into how library access and services have impacted other areas of the university. Information literacy is one area of overlap between library access and services and the university's curriculum, and the self-study process brings new information to light about how the library's information literacy initiatives have impacted the curriculum. Integrating information literacy into the university's degree programs is one of the library's goals. Progress toward this goal is tracked and assessed through data collected by the library in the monthly review cycle: how many courses have an embedded librarian, how many class presentations are given each semester, which courses utilize library resources, and which courses are good candidates for deeper engagement with library resources. New information added to this data during the self-study include student artifacts, which are assessed to determine if the students are achieving the learning goals of key courses in the degree programs. Since these are collected by the faculty and are maintained by the academic dean's office, the library has not had access to these assignments and artifacts from the students.

Conversations about the self-study reveal many parallels between student artifact assessment and the library's report on its progress toward the goal of integrating information literacy into the university's degree programs. Artifacts from many of the courses with embedded librarians received higher marks for meeting course goals related to information literacy, indicating that the library's embedded librarian program is working. Artifacts from courses that the library had identified as being good candidates for deeper engagement with library resources were particularly enlightening. Based on the assessment rubric used by the faculty for the self-study, some of those courses were meeting the learning objectives for information literacy without any additional library support. Other courses, however, clearly show room for improving student learning in information literacy. The self-study assessment of student artifacts also prompts new ideas and brainstorms for how the library might support information literacy learning goals in courses not previously targeted for deeper library engagement, as well as new ways to partner with faculty in teaching information literacy. The library director, open to the self-study process, is now able to adjust the library's integrated plan to incorporate new ideas based on the findings of the self-study process. When the accreditation team visits and meets with the library director, they are impressed by how the findings from the self-study are already being worked into new outcomes and actions for the integrated plan.

Summary

This chapter looked at how a library's integrated plan matures through long-term assessment and adjustment. This is a crucial component of Integrated Library Planning because it keeps your planning process moving forward, informed by everything that is going on both around and within the library. In particular, this chapter focused on how to strategically respond to observations of information behavior, the role of financial review in decision making, ways to add new action plans to a rolling horizon, when and how to revise goals and strategic outcomes, and the value of integrating external review cycles.

Incorporating what you learn from observing information behavior needs to be done strategically, not reactively. Additional research and evaluation are often needed to determine the specific information need and how it relates to the library's mission and vision. Incorporating an emerging information need into the integrated plan requires matching it with an appropriate goal and strategic outcome. If one does not already exist in the integrated plan, look for ways to update the plan. There might be ways to update existing goals and outcomes to be more inclusive of the emerging information need, or perhaps the need warrants the addition of a new goal or strategic outcome. Once action plans are created, it is possible to begin tracking the library's progress toward meeting emerging information needs.

Library operations are mercilessly tied to budgets and, therefore, an integrated plan must take the financial impact of its action plans into account as part of the planning process. While there may be occasions when a new action plan has a small budgetary impact, most new action plans added to an integrated plan need funding to move forward. An action plan's funding requirements may determine when it is scheduled on the rolling horizon and whether fundraising needs to be added to the scope of the action plan. The information collected in the monthly review cycle to support action plans can be used to propose budgets inclusive of appropriate funding and to inform smart spending of budget surpluses.

When planning on a rolling horizon, it is tempting to simply add new plans to the months that are tacked onto the end of the horizon as it rolls. Integrated Library Planning, with its continual assessment, offers an opportunity to reposition and shift action plans on the rolling horizon as change occurs. It is important to keep questions about timing, priority, dependency, and workload impact at the forefront when reviewing the rolling horizon. Placing new action plans on a rolling horizon might involve matching it with a related action plan or replacing an action plan that is no longer needed. Keeping an eye on workload balance in relation to the library's rhythms is also critically important. Adjustments to the rolling horizon may be made when action plans fall behind. If completion of action plans falls behind consistently, reevaluating how much time is allocated for each action plan might be helpful in reestablishing reasonable expectations.

Revising goals and strategic outcomes is essential for keeping the integrated plan relevant and responsive. This can be done when all the action plans under an outcome are complete but does not often happen in clearly defined ways. As new action plans are added under strategic outcomes and goals, some shifting will occur over time. Regularly looking at goals and strategic outcomes in relation to their action plans helps you identify when a significant shift has occurred that warrants updating or revising the outcome or goal. Moments when a library experiences a major shift in workflow or changes in staffing are also opportunities to revisit goals and strategic outcomes. These are changes that you can make to an integrated plan when the timing is appropriate.

Most libraries participate in external review cycles determined by their parent institution. The monthly review cycle can be designed to streamline reporting data for external review. An integrated plan can also incorporate findings and feedback from an external review into new action plans and revised goals and strategic outcomes. Attending to this two-way flow of information in a responsible way is important for the integrity of both the integrated plan and the external review process. Engaging in an external review cycle informed by comprehensive data collected through the monthly review cycle can lead to powerful new insights for the integrated plan.

CHAPTER 7

Stepping into an Integrated Future

Once a library's integrated plan enters the fourth stage, it is tempting to lean back and let the plan take off, working on automatic pilot. However, because an integrated plan has no fixed timeframe, it is when the plan reaches its maturity that the planner becomes more involved monitoring progress and identifying when adjustments need to be made. Having a plan without a fixed end date might seem daunting or frightening, or perhaps it sparks doubt and skepticism. How can an ongoing, perpetual planning cycle operating on a rolling horizon ever result in any measurable outcomes? How will it stay fresh and relevant? Is the monthly review cycle robust enough to keep the plan current? A time may come when the plan falls short and the library stalls in its progress toward its goals. When this happens, Integrated Library Planning offers the chance to make adaptations and move in a new direction. For those who like to be able to see a finish line and are accustomed to having a defined completion point with traditional strategic plans, stepping into an integrated future presents an opportunity to redefine what it means to reach a finish line.

The integrated plan at Lancaster Theological Seminary Library has been in use for over seven years. It outlasted two institutional strategic plans, helped the library pass a focused visit from an accreditation team, and informed many innovations and positive developments. A fair number of challenges have arisen, and the library has experienced more than a few disruptions during this time. The plan has weathered it all. The more the plan has needed to flex or adapt to the current situation, the stronger it has become. Integrated Library Planning is resilient, a quality especially valuable at a time when uncertainties are increasing. Through the long-term implementation of our integrated plan, I have learned new habits, helping me continue to develop the plan and become a more resilient

Personal Narrative: Fruits of Integrated Library Planning

Lancaster Theological Seminary Library implemented its monthly review cycle in July 2015. It was preceded by nine months of foundation and groundwork with a few additional months spent on developing the planning structure and creating the format for the monthly review report. It was the start of a new fiscal year, and I had also conducted an annual review of the previous year to support the new monthly review cycle. I made slight adjustments to the monthly review report format each month to make it more concise and easier to read. Three months into the plan, it was clear we needed to make some substantial adjustments. The monthly review cycle did not quite match the rhythms of the library; therefore, the cycle was revised, and the timing of each activity was rescheduled to match scheduled monthly meetings and workload fluctuation.

By the ninth month we were ready to make adjustments to the way operational areas were organized. As a small library with a small staff, the operational areas in our plan were organized in a way that complemented our mission and vision statements. Since the library's staff members often share responsibilities across functionally diverse operational areas, it did not make sense to organize the plan in a way that complemented staff deployment. However, as I engaged in monthly review, I saw that several of our operational areas shared similar goals. Continuing to conduct assessments and planning for multiple related areas was inefficient. To give us more space to conduct a reorganization of the integrated plan, the April 2016 monthly review cycle extended to include May, making it a two-month review report. We decided to consolidate three operational areas into one, bringing their respective goals under one area. We also made several updates to strategic outcomes and goals of the other areas. These adjustments were prompted by a variety of circumstances: recognizing areas where the plan could be more concise, updating language to reflect changes in the seminary's policy and adoption of a new mission statement, and pairing goals and outcomes with an appropriate operational area to reflect more accurately what the library hoped to achieve.

The monthly review cycle continued without any further major changes for the next academic year. The library was scheduled to receive a focused visit from an accreditation team for the Association of Theological Schools in March 2017 as a follow-up to the seminary's reaccreditation in spring of 2014, immediately before I was hired. I found the monthly review reports extremely helpful when preparing my report for the team. I was able to share the details of our integrated plan, which action plans we had completed, and the progress we were making toward our goals and outcomes. I was also able to tell them what we were learning about the library's patrons and how these observations informed our plan. The outcome of the visit was successful, and the library was commended for its preparation, organization, and forward-thinking plan.

When I was granted a six-month sabbatical in the second half of 2017, it was not realistic to pass the responsibility of compiling monthly reviews to my only full-time library staff member, who would already be shouldering a heavy burden in my absence. The monthly review cycle would simply have to be delayed until my return. I arranged to spend two days per month in the library to check in with the staff and attend to administrative tasks that could not be delegated. I also used this time to monitor the action plans that were scheduled during those months of the rolling planning horizon and made copious notes of things to look at in more detail when my sabbatical ended. Upon my return, I compiled a biannual review report that included six months of assessments and observations, and our eighteen-month rolling planning horizon lurched ahead by a third of its length. It was not ideal, but the review showed that the library still made progress toward its goals and outcomes during that time. While we were not innovating much or responding to emerging information needs during that time, we had not stopped our observations and were ready to resume that aspect of the plan in 2018.

The next significant change to the integrated plan was an expansive revision and restructure that we finalized in April 2019. It was the culmination of several significant changes that had occurred over time, including a major library staff reorganization and the start of a new strategic planning cycle for the seminary. It was also time to update the mission and vision statements to be inclusive of new responsibilities assigned to the library, like oversight of the learning management system. I realized the need to revisit some of the deep work we did to develop the plan in the fall of 2018 and worked diligently on that as we continued the monthly review cycle. I convened meetings and conversation groups with library, writing center, and learning management support staff so that all these perspectives could inform the plan's revision. We thoroughly rewrote the library's mission and vision statements and redefined the library's organizational structure to align with the new statements. We also clarified the different levels of the integrated plan and how the monthly review cycle would work. Each operational area now had a single goal that stemmed directly from the mission and vision statements, and strategic outcomes were rewritten to represent achievable and completable outcomes. The monthly review reports would measure and track progress toward strategic outcomes, simplifying our previous reports which had tracked and reported progress on individual action plans. Action plans were still mapped onto the eighteen-month rolling horizon, but the overall monthly review was streamlined significantly by these changes. We also changed the format of the information behavior analysis section so that we could better track new trends, trends we were watching, and action plans we created to address needs waiting to be scheduled on the rolling horizon.

The impacts of our integrated plan range from small, slight improvements to major developments that have had effects beyond our immediate communities. Within the first year of implementation, we noticed recurring reference questions coming from our patrons. Many of the questions seemed relatively straightforward, yet most of them were being referred to the librarian or other senior staff. Regular monitoring and assessment of our reference tracking tool also revealed that student staff were not always providing complete or correct answers to simple questions. This led us to identify a gap in our student worker training: they had not been trained or coached how to handle reference interviews. Once we identified this, we were able to create appropriate action plans under an existing strategic outcome and schedule its completion on the rolling planning horizon. When student workers received the new reference interview training and were given electronic access to additional training resources and library documentation that had previously only been provided in print format, we noticed improvement in the quality of our reference services.

One major improvement made possible through our integrated plan was a reallocation and redesign of our public spaces in the summer of 2019. Work toward achieving this outcome coincided with a goal to reduce the circulating collection to a sustainable size. Over the course of three years, I consulted with my faculty colleagues to review holdings that had not circulated in the past twenty years. This resulted in removal of approximately thirty-five percent of our collection. By the time we pulled everything identified for deaccessioning, it was clear we had more shelving than we needed. While the seminary had not yet determined another use for the space, we sent out several surveys to our patrons asking about the library's spaces. We also walked through the library periodically over the course of a month to observe how patrons used our spaces. This feedback then informed our new plans for the space. Plush chairs for solitary study in our quiet spaces are spaced apart from each other to create more privacy, now with reading lamps and power supplies. We sold our small study carrel desks and replaced them with large tables set apart by room dividers so that students can spread out their books, notebooks, and computers in a semi-secluded space that promotes better focus. Our patrons were often confused by the way the stacks were organized on our lower floor, so we took the opportunity to rearrange them for easier navigation. Furniture on our main floor, where we encourage conversation and gatherings, was replaced with café tables and a custom sectional seating piece more conducive to the purpose of the space. All these improvements were informed by what we learned through our Integrated Library Planning and were completed on time with the help of the monthly review cycle.

Another area of library operation that has seen significant innovation through Integrated Library Planning is our library systems. Recall from chapter 2 that the library system in use when I arrived at Lancaster Theological Seminary was the same one that had been in place since the library automated in 1996. While our integrated plan was under development, we migrated the library's catalog to Koha in December 2014. That was the beginning of a series of upgrades and improvements aimed to improve our patron experience and online presence. Student surveys consistently revealed frustration over having to conduct searches in multiple places: the library catalog and each of our databases. As I developed our electronic collections, a discovery service began to make sense to address our patrons' woes. When presented with an opportunity to adopt a discovery service integrated with Koha, meaning that our patrons would not have to learn a new interface so soon after being introduced to Koha, our research and findings from the monthly review cycle aided us in the decision. As we implemented the new discovery service, we received and monitored feedback from our students and faculty, who experienced frustration with accessing full-text search results off campus. Because we used referring URL technology for most of our remote authentication, off-campus access was extraordinarily clunky. When the opportunity arose to become early adopters of a single-sign-on solution for remote authentication directly integrated with Koha, we were confident in taking that chance. As a result, our testing of and feedback on the new plugin, which was deeply informed by our familiarity with what our patrons needed, has been valuable to the developers and has aided the ongoing development of a service now used by libraries worldwide. Our library played a similarly valuable role as early adopters of the Elasticsearch search engine when it became integrated into Koha. Knowledge gained through the monthly review cycle of how our patrons use the catalog and what they would expect to see when they execute a search helped us to map the MARC fields we use for local notes, create a custom search index, and assign weights to search fields. This pioneering work informed a template within Koha now used by many academic libraries migrating to Koha with Elasticsearch.

Balancing Observation, Analysis, and Assessment

While I can attribute many accomplishments of the Lancaster Theological Seminary Library to Integrated Library Planning, I recognize that simply following the monthly review cycle and compiling monthly review reports did not produce these results by themselves. Rather, the act of following the monthly review cycle and compiling monthly review reports prompted me to develop additional habits that help me process, interpret, and innovate for the library and its patrons. The foremost habit I have worked on cultivating is that of finding balance between observation, analysis, and assessment.

Assessment is at the center of the monthly review cycle. Engaging in assessment each month is unavoidable, and the monthly review report is essentially an assessment report for the integrated plan with financial review and some observational analysis thrown in. The perpetual and cyclical nature of monthly review makes it very easy to stay in assessment mode all the time. While assessment is a good way of tracking and improving the plan, it is not helpful to be laser focused on only what is currently going on in the plan. To keep the plan fresh, you need to acquire new knowledge and insights about the library, its patrons, and what is going on around the library. Therefore, the monthly review cycle requires an equal amount of observation and analysis to accompany the assessment so that new information can be fed into the plan as it moves forward.

Observation, specifically observing information behavior and forming strategic responses to it, was covered in the previous chapter. This is one of the most important activities you can do during the monthly review cycle. Watching what your patrons do, watching your library staff, watching what circulates, watching how the library's websites and social media accounts are used—these are all very important activities, offering insights and sparking ideas to improve the library. Specifically, analyzing observations helps to make connections between observing the behavior, determining what the information need is, and crafting the library's response. In our integrated plan, however, we tend to use the same data for assessing what is going on in the plan and for observing what is happening in and around the library. Using the same data for two different purposes can be tricky. The unfortunate result is that the information behavior analysis section of the monthly review report has not received the attention it deserves.

Our library's monthly review cycle, in its original design, included a space for observations to be shared at the library staff meeting. These observations, questions, and suggestions received from patrons would then be recorded and analyzed to determine if they could or should be turned into action plans and added to the rolling horizon. This was the ideal. In reality, two or three observations were shared initially during our meetings, which soon decreased to one or two. Then, our library staff meetings became irregular for various reasons. I could not leave a giant hole in the monthly review report where observed information behavior analysis should be, so I began looking for other sources of data that could offer similar insights. Over time, our monthly review report began including statistics of reference interviews, website visits, social media engagement, catalog searches, and more. All these statistics informed assessments of our progress toward our goals and outcome for providing quality reference services, improving our patrons' online experience, promoting library collections and services, and curating a collection that supports teaching and learning. Yet they could also tell me if the same question was being asked by multiple people, if there were pages on our website that were more popular than others, and which keywords and other types of searches our patrons used, for example. While we were not directly observing our patrons' information behavior in the way I had originally intended, the data gathered for assessment also told us something about information behavior—if we asked different questions when we looked at it.

When I first discovered this, I thought it was a near-perfect solution. Using data for both assessment and to glean observations would ensure that there was always something to consider each month for observed information behavior analysis. We would always have a source of information that could suggest if an emerging need or trend was present that might need an innovation or change in direction. What I have found, however, is that it is not a substitute for firsthand observation of our patrons, nor can it adequately replace what happens in a library staff meeting when we share feedback we have received from patrons or questions we have been asked. It is still the case that during some months all I have for observed information behavior analysis are the insights I get from the data and statistics collected for assessment. However, the months in which the library staff share insights from firsthand accounts give the analysis a little more depth, a little more life. It does not always work out that way as some months are busier than others, and sometimes we remember more to share with each other than at other times. It is a matter of balance, though. When we achieve that balance between observation, analysis, and assessment, the integrated plan improves and the library benefits.

Overcoming Inevitable Challenges

Implementing Integrated Library Planning is not without its share of challenges. Since the development and implementation of our integrated plan, our library has experienced an array of difficulties, delays, and unforeseen troubles. By facing and overcoming these situations, I have learned that Integrated Library Planning is truly flexible, dynamic, and responsive. Challenges are disruptive and often threaten traditional strategic plans that are more fixed by nature. Because of the way an integrated plan is designed, with a monthly review cycle affording planners an opportunity to revise, reschedule, or change direction, it can adapt to challenge much more readily than other types of planning. This adaptability creates a built-in capacity for resilience. In turn, as a library leader who oversees an integrated plan, I learn to become more resilient as the library faces and overcomes challenges.

Challenges come from a variety of sources. Some challenges originate from the plan itself. As the plan moves into implementation phase, it takes time to calibrate and for the planning team to learn how to work with the monthly review cycle. One of the biggest recurring challenges for me is scheduling action plans on the rolling planning horizon. I have discovered that this is an art that needs to be practiced. When done well, everything runs smoothly, and the work environment is relatively happy and peaceful from a planning perspective. When it is not done well, everything is hectic, and the work environment is more stressed and agitated. Sometimes a project has not been given enough time for completion; deadlines are missed and the duration of the project has to be extended, impacting the scheduling of other action plans. Sometimes too many action plans are scheduled at the same time, forcing heavier workloads for staff when projects under an external deadline cannot be moved or extended. Try as I might to avoid both scenarios, they will inevitably happen.

After experiencing this type of challenge repeatedly, I have realized that this is not a failing of my ability to effectively schedule nor is it a failing of the integrated plan. This is how life is. Sometimes something just takes a little longer to complete, and sometimes we must take on extra work to meet deadlines. However, Integrated Library Planning and a monthly review cycle do help by highlighting those times and offering space to prepare and reflect on what happened so that it might be improved the next time the library is in a similar situation. Our rolling planning horizon is set for eighteen months, allowing us to look ahead and adjust projects that recur on an annual basis when what we have learned from the current year is fresh in our minds. The rolling planning horizon can also alert planners that a particularly busy or hectic time is approaching. Even if it is not possible to redistribute action plans and projects to avoid the overload, knowing that it is coming helps everyone prepare and cope with it.

Challenge can also originate from within the library, or within the library's environment. These are the unanticipated changes or disruptions that are not on the planning horizon. It could be a building issue, like a roof leak or electrical problem. Or it could be a library system issue. The biggest challenges I have faced originating from within the library have been related to staffing. As director of a small library with a small staff, any change in staffing is incredibly disruptive. More often than not, the change is also unanticipated. Every time we say good-bye to a staff member, it sets off a chain reaction of events eventually impacting almost every area of library operation.

Just as challenge can originate from within the library, it can also originate from external sources. The ultimate example of this is the COVID-19 pandemic and crisis. There are more ordinary external challenges as well: new standards from an accreditor that need to be woven into the plan, changes in enrollment or population, and decisions made by others having a direct effect on the library. As with changes or disruptions originating from within the library, some of these external challenges we anticipate and plan for while others we cannot. For those disruptions that we see coming, the time to prepare is valuable and an integrated plan can be part of that preparation. Unfortunately, there is not always time to prepare before a disruption is fully present. For example, how many libraries had pandemic procedures included in their library's emergency preparedness plan prior to COVID-19?

When experiencing challenges, both internal and external, I have found the integrated plan to be a source of support. As chaos and uncertainty swirl around the library, the integrated plan can be a grounding reminder of the library's identity and purpose. When we have lost a staff member, the integrated plan helps me visualize and understand the adaptations we need to make until the vacancy is filled. The integrated plan has also helped me quickly assess whether we want to fill the same position or if there is an opportunity to redefine the vacancy to match the library's needs more closely. At a time when emotions and stress are high, having the integrated plan and its rich trove of research and assessment is invaluable when faced with high-impact decisions. In the case of

COVID-19, the integrated plan was a go-to resource to quickly recalibrate the library's services. I was able to go through each operational area asking what could continue during the shutdown, what our patrons would need during the shutdown, and what we must pause or cancel. What could have been overwhelming turned into a manageable opportunity to reimagine how the library might continue to fulfill its mission during a pandemic shutdown. Energy that could have been spent assessing the situation and replanning went directly into finding solutions for a mostly remote workforce and developing contact-free checkout and pickup services.

Integrated Library Planning is a set of practices that has empowered me to become a more resilient library leader. By its design, I feel I always have ready access to the information I need to make good decisions in times of crisis and change. In the times when I do not get it right, when the decision was not the best one for the moment or the plan itself is a barrier to the library performing optimally, the monthly review cycle gives me another opportunity to make an adjustment, correct the course, and try again. Overcoming challenges in and with an integrated plan involves learning from them, building resilience, and finding the courage to keep moving forward.

Recognizing and Celebrating Accomplishments

One final habit I would like to share that I have learned through the implementation of our integrated plan is the importance of recognizing the library's accomplishments and celebrating them. The monthly review cycle does not lend itself well to this habit. It is something that the planning team needs to intentionally bring to it. By doing so, the acts of recognition and celebration boost library staff morale, potentially raising job satisfaction and increasing productivity. Notable accomplishments the library chooses to share and celebrate widely have a positive impact on the community's perception of the library.

To be successful in this habit requires discipline and mindfulness. The monthly review cycle and rolling planning horizon create a rhythm that carries a lot of forward momentum. It is the engine of the integrated plan and is extraordinarily powerful and effective for the plan and the library. One of the not-so-positive side effects of this rhythm, however, is that it encourages constant forward motion with little rest. While time for reflection and assessment is also part of the monthly review cycle, the relatively brief period for review (typically one month) and the repetitive cycle keep pushing the library forward to the next thing when projects are completed and outcomes are achieved.

Taking a moment to pause, step back, and appreciate what has been accomplished through an integrated plan can be incredibly restorative. There is a time and place for allowing the rolling planning horizon to sweep the library along a path toward the future. This can be the land of dreams and ambitions, inspiration and innovation. There is also a time for rest, to settle into an awareness of the present, and to appreciate where the library is and what has led it to this particular place and time. Parties are fun and bonuses are appreciated by staff. These are important signs and symbols of recognition. However, it is equally important to provide a little space for a mindful awareness of the library's accomplishments and a celebration of that from a deeper place.

I am still trying to incorporate this habit into our integrated plan and monthly review cycle. At the end of the fiscal year, the monthly review report I compile also includes an annual summary. The template I have created for our monthly review reports includes but hides the annual summary sections until I need them, so I am able to add content to those sections throughout the year and make them visible when the fiscal year ends. I strive to give attention to each outcome achieved over the course of the year, offering thanks and appreciation to those who contributed to its successful completion. It is a moment to pause and reflect, not for the purposes of assessment or to consider ways to improve but simply for the purposes of appreciation, thankfulness, and celebration.

Final Thoughts

The integrated plan at the Lancaster Theological Seminary Library has been in place for more than seven years. While that may be considered a long time to operate under a traditional strategic plan, I believe our integrated plan has remained relevant and continues to serve the library and our patrons well. We have been able to restructure the library's operational areas to adjust to new institutional responsibilities, and we have been able to revise our strategic outcomes, goals, mission, and vision when the timing was appropriate instead of forced. The integrated plan provides us with information about the library's performance and the changing environment around the library. Although we have adapted the monthly review cycle and tweaked the plan's processes more than once, the integrated plan continues to help the library achieve its potential and respond to emerging needs proactively. I do not feel a need to adopt a different model of planning.

Integrated Library Planning has also helped me to become a more effective library leader. It has fueled my creativity and given me space to explore and innovate. I am also learning new habits from operating with an integrated plan. I am learning how to balance assessment with observation and analysis, how to become more resilient by facing and overcoming challenge, and how to take time to recognize and celebrate accomplishments. I believe that the best style of planning is the one that empowers you to both become and achieve more than you would without it. This is what Integrated Library Planning is for me and for the library I lead.

Integrated Library Planning is not easy. It takes a lot of time and attention. It is a demanding style of planning and management for libraries. But this is a demanding time and age for libraries. Our libraries, institutions, and organizations are experiencing fast-paced change coupled with social, economic, and political uncertainty exceeding that of previous generations. All indications suggest that changes will continue at a fast pace, and uncertainty will persist. Though it is not easy, I believe Integrated Library Planning is what this moment calls for. As a model, it has the capacity to integrate the best tools and practices of library leadership and management while supporting growth, innovation, and resilience. Embrace change, take courage, and leap into an integrated future.

Acknowledgments

This book is dedicated to all the public library and school librarians who made me feel at home in their libraries as I was growing up in Corsicana and Mesquite, Texas. Especially Mrs. Fisk. You cultivated within me a love for libraries and a passion for their potential to tell powerful stories, preserve uncomfortable truths, and spark change in the world.

This book would not have been possible without the support and encouragement of many people. I would like to thank, first and foremost, the staff members of the Lancaster Theological Seminary Library from 2014 to 2022. Each of them contributed something to the development of Integrated Library Planning through their ideas, questions, and support. This includes full-time library associates Katie Cort, Hannah Bingman, Tim Whitney, Peggy O'Kane, and Chynaah Maryoung-Cooke; part-time library assistants Elizabeth Gates, Janice Herman, Audrey Skilton, and Rose Shepley; and student assistants Naomi Leapheart-Washington, Harum "RJ" Ulmer, Fa Lane, Philip Anglin, Dumas Thompson, Joao Teixeira, Amy Fishburn, Kellie Turner, Jeffery Caldwell, Kelsey Wallace, Linda Peachey, Katie Jackson, Mark Harris, Megan Mathieson, Kecia Munroe, Marion Smith, David Fehr, Michael Bright, Eli Elisha, Mwat Asedeh, and John Brewster. I am also extraordinarily grateful to my writing center colleagues—Frank Gray and Brian McDonald—and colleagues who assisted me with learning management system support—Augustine Apprey and Michael Wilson.

I would also like to give special thanks to Elizabeth Palmer Bennett, Lancaster Seminary's Vice President for Finance and Administration and Chief Financial Officer from 2012 to 2021, and my direct supervisor. Her mentorship, guidance, and counsel has been a cornerstone of my professional development over the past eight years. She was a conversation partner through every challenge the library faced, patient listener to all my wild ideas, and powerful backer as we recentered the library in campus life. She not only read my monthly review reports for six years but engaged with them by asking questions and challenging assumptions.

130   Acknowledgments

It has been an honor and a privilege to serve on the most supportive and affirming faculty in theological education. My faculty colleagues are advocates for the library and partners in information literacy education. They have encouraged and affirmed my growth as a librarian, an administrator, a faculty member, and a scholar. I give my humble thanks and appreciation to Lee Barrett, Greg Carey, Stephanie Crumpton, Anabel Proffitt, Julia O'Brien, Anne Thayer, and Catherine Williams. Thank you to David Mellott, Vice President of Academic Affairs and Dean until 2019, who placed a lot of trust and confidence in me and my ability to provide leadership for both the library and the learning management system. I am also grateful to Dean Vanessa Lovelace who stepped in as academic dean in 2019 and became a colleague who shares my vision for what a library can be, and to Dean Heather Vacek who is a new advocate as the Lancaster Theological Seminary Library relocates itself within Moravian University. I would also like to give thanks to the administration of Lancaster Seminary, particularly President Carol Lytch, Interim President David Rowe, and the trustees of the seminary who affirmed my desire to write this book and granted me two sabbaticals to complete the manuscript.

Several colleagues in Atla, the membership organization formerly known as the American Theological Library Association, provided feedback and encouragement to me as I have developed Integrated Library Planning. Thank you to Kelly Campbell, Susan Ebertz, James Estes, Douglas Gragg, and Andrew Keck. I would also like to thank my Association of Theological Schools Women in Leadership mentoring cohort for their unfailing support and affirmation: Esther Menn, Alex Macias, and Leslie Ortiz.

Integrated Library Planning would not have come to be if it were not for those who introduced me to some influential and inspiring thoughts. I owe a debt of gratitude to Linda Swaine at Florida State University for introducing me to the writings of Margaret Wheatley in her library leadership courses. I am also deeply indebted to Kevin Fitzgerald and his assistant Maureen Moloney, who provided me with an employment opportunity at Mondelēz International that taught me about Integrated Business Planning firsthand. Although I did not realize it at the time, these experiences were transformational for me and shaped the way in which I understand organizations, leadership, strategy, and planning.

Thank you to Erin Nevius and her team at ACRL Publications. Erin was extremely patient and understanding as I completed my manuscript. It has been a pleasure to work with you to see this project through to its completion.

Finally, I would like to give my deepest thanks and gratitude to my family, who have journeyed with me through this process. To my parents for their unconditional love and support, to my parents-in-law for their encouragement and understanding, and to my siblings-in-law for their companionship and camaraderie. To my devoted husband Darryl, for the hours he spent offering feedback on my manuscript and for years of support, encouragement, and love. To our two exceptional teenagers, Zeke and Cecily, I hardly have the words to convey the depth of my love and appreciation for you. You are each a source of joy that has kept me grounded and moving forward through the toughest times. Thank you, thank you; a thousand times, thank you.

APPENDIX A

Helpful Resources and Tools

Hosting Conversations

Art of Hosting

https://artofhosting.org/
This is an international community of practitioners interested in the "art of hosting and harvesting conversations that matter." The website provides a comprehensive overview of the Art of Hosting and the methods it employs, provides a range of resources, and connects practitioners around the world.

The Circle Way

https://www.thecircleway.net/
This is a facilitated conversational method that arranges people in a circle and observes a set of rules designed to promote equality and respect among the participants. The website tells this history of the Circle Way and offers many resources for learning more.

The World Café

http://www.theworldcafe.com
This is a method for hosting and facilitating large group discussions by using rounds. Participants are divided into small groups who rotate among tables discussing a new question during each round. The website introduces the

133

principles of the World Café methodology, provides free resources and a store, and offers training opportunities.

Open Space Technology

https://openspaceworld.org/wp2/
This is a method for running productive meetings that is suitable for any size group, any kind of organization, and any type of meeting. The structure is determined by the people participating in the meetings and the type of ideas involved. This website is the home for practitioners of Open Space Technology and those who want to learn more. It is translated into many languages and connects an international community.

Appreciative Inquiry

https://appreciativeinquiry.champlain.edu/
This is a method of strategic planning that helps organizations shift their perspective and focus on strengths and opportunities that can lead to positive organizational change. The website includes an overview of the method, resources and videos, success stories, and opportunities to connect with a global community of practitioners.

Mind Mapping and Diagramming

Freeplane

https://www.freeplane.org/wiki/index.php/Home
Open-source mind mapping application with an active development and support community. It requires Java to run. It has a wide range of functions including a presentation mode.

XMind

https://www.xmind.net/
Full-featured mind mapping application with desktop, mobile, and web browser access. Available for Windows, macOS, Linux, iOS, and Android. A free trial download is available; to license it, there is special pricing available for academic institutions and governmental organizations.

MindMeister

https://www.mindmeister.com/
Online mind mapping website with no software to download. The free tier allows up to three mind maps and includes collaboration features. To export or print, a paid subscription is required.

Coggle

https://coggle.it/
Another online, cloud-based mind mapping application. Free tier allows up to three private diagrams and unlimited public diagrams, along with image upload, export, download, and embed capabilities.

Gantt Charts

Gantt Chart Spreadsheet Templates

https://extensions.libreoffice.org/en/extensions/show/gantt-chart-template
https://templates.office.com/en-us/simple-gantt-chart-tm16400962
Fancy software or web sites are not required for creating functional Gantt charts. These free templates, one from the LibreOffice community and one from Microsoft Office, make it easy to use a spreadsheet application to create a Gantt chart.

GanttProject

https://www.ganttproject.biz/
Open-source Gantt chart application that runs on Windows, macOS, and Linux. Simple and straightforward interface for single-user project tracking.

ProjectLibre

https://www.projectlibre.com/
Open-source project management application designed to compete with Microsoft Project and available for Windows, macOS, and Linux. In addition to creating Gantt charts, this application also produces network diagrams, histograms, and more.

Instagantt

https://instagantt.com/
Cloud-based Gantt chart creator that integrates with Asana, a popular project management website. A seven-day free trial is available; requires a subscription for unlimited use.

Project Management

Taiga

https://www.taiga.io/ and https://github.com/taigaio
An open-source project management tool that has both hosted and self-hosted options. It includes planning tools, communication pathways, statistics, and more. It includes both Kanban board and scrum interfaces and is highly customizable.

Asana

https://asana.com/
Cloud-based collaborative project management and project planning website. Create unlimited project boards, assign tasks to coworkers, specify due dates, and more. Basic plans are free, and premium features require a paid subscription.

Trello

https://trello.com/
Cloud-based collaborative project management app that utilizes Kanban boards, along with list and card views. Also includes team collaboration tools. The free plan is limited to ten boards.

Airtable

https://airtable.com
Cloud-based project management solution that is highly flexible and customizable. Organize workflows into workspaces, bases, and tables. Create multiple views for tables and link records across tables. The free plan includes access for five creators or editors and 1,200 records per base.

ClickUp

https://clickup.com/

A cloud-based collaborative project management app that combines features from both Asana and Trello. Highly customizable project boards, supports collaborative documents, and offers a real-time chat feature. The free plan is limited to 100 MB of cloud storage space.

APPENDIX B

Sample Report Outlines

These sample report outlines offer a suggestion for how to organize and structure the information that is collected when developing an integrated library plan and during the monthly review cycle. They may be adapted to fit a library's preference in terms of layout, style, and format. Libraries and their parent institutions may have templates and brand guides that will direct the layout and style of reports. A text document or a slide presentation are two popular formats that may be used.

Initial Report for an Integrated Library Plan

It is helpful to record and compile all the work that is completed in the first two stages of an integrated library plan, when the library completes its preparation and groundwork, and the planning structure is developed. Not all of this information will be carried over to the monthly review report. This document will serve as a reference for the entire integrated library plan once it is implemented.

I. Introduction
II. Background information
   A. Links or citations to official documents
   B. Additional information compiled and not previously documented
III. Mission and vision statements
   A. Mission and vision statements of the parent institution
   B. Previous library mission and vision statements
   C. New library mission and vision statements
IV. Needs assessment
   A. Division or operational area 1

140   Appendix B

       1. Role and function of the division or operational area
       2. Summary of findings from needs assessment relating to the division or operational area
   B. Division or operational area 2, etc. (follow template as above, repeat as needed)

V. Strengths, weaknesses, opportunities, and threats
   A. SWOT matrix
   B. Additional explanatory information (optional)

VI. Operational areas, goals, and strategic outcomes
   A. List of all operational areas, grouped by division if applicable
   B. Operational area 1
       1. Goal
       2. Strategic outcomes
   C. Operational area 2, etc. (follow template as above, repeat as needed)
   D. Mapping of goals and outcomes to external standards (optional)

VII. Starter action plans
   A. Operational area 1
       1. Action plan 1, include list of tasks and target completion date
       2. Action plan 2, etc. (repeat as needed)
   B. Operational area 2, etc. (follow template as above, repeat as needed)
   C. Gantt chart or other tool to show action plan scheduling

VIII. Monthly review cycle
   A. Overview of each component and schedule of planning activities for the month
   B. Process summary describes in depth the entire month's planning activities
   C. Components to be included in the monthly review report

Monthly Review Report, Variation 1

This sample outline for a monthly review report is for a library that has two levels of organization for library operation: division and operational area. It can be adapted to remove the division level if the library has only one level of organization. The information needs and behavior analysis is included in a section

Sample Report Outlines 141

separate from the assessment sections. Statistical data related to operational area assessment is recorded in the assessment sections, while additional statistical data collected for determining needs is recorded in the information behavior analysis section. The report closes with an updated rolling horizon planning map, along with a summary of revisions to goals, strategic outcomes, and action plans.

I.   Division 1 assessment
    A. Operational area 1
        1. Status of strategic outcomes and action plans
        2. Tasks completed
        3. Statistical data related to tasks completed
    B. Operational area 2, etc. (follow template as above, repeat as needed)
II.   Division 2 assessment, etc. (follow template as above, repeat as needed)
III.   Financial summary
    A. Expenditures
    B. Income
    C. Fiscal year budget status
IV.   Information needs and behavior analysis
    A. Relevant reports and statistics
    B. Recorded observations
    C. Identified needs
V.   Goals, strategic outcomes, and action plans
    A. Planning horizon overview with mapped action plans
    B. Revisions to goals
    C. Revisions to strategic outcomes
    D. Any other revisions to the integrated library plan to be documented

Monthly Review Report, Variation 2

Like the first variation, this outline reflects two levels of library operation and can be adapted to suit a library that only uses one level for organizational purposes. The mission and vision statements, along with an organizational chart for library operations, are included at the beginning of the report. Goals and strategic outcomes are placed in the assessment sections. Instead of one master rolling horizon planning map, it is split by operational area and included in the assessment section, which can be laid out like a series of dashboard reports if desired. For libraries that use data for both assessment and information behavior analysis, all statistical data is collected into one section for operational data. The information behavior analysis section focuses on naming trends newly identified, trends watched for potential development, and action plans developed but not yet scheduled onto the rolling planning horizon.

I. Mission and vision statement, including any revisions (if applicable)
II. Library organization chart, including any revisions (if applicable)
III. Division 1 assessment
    A. Goals for all operational areas in the division
    B. Operational area 1
        1. Status of strategic outcomes and tasks completed
        2. Updated rolling horizon planning map
    C. Operational area 2, etc. (follow template as above, repeat as needed)
IV. Division 2 assessment, etc. (follow template as above, repeat as needed)
V. Financial summary
    A. Expenditures
    B. Income
    C. Fiscal year budget status
VI. Operational data
    A. Statistical data related to the tasks completed for the month
    B. Charts that put this month's statistics into historical context
VII. Information behavior analysis
    A. Division 1
        1. New trends
        2. Watch list
        3. Action plans waiting to be scheduled on the planning horizon
    B. Division 2, etc. (follow template as above, repeat as needed)

Bibliography

ACRL Research Planning and Review Committee. *2021 Environmental Scan.* Association of College and Research Libraries, April 2021. https://www.ala.org/acrl/sites/ala.org.acrl/files/content/publications/whitepapers/EnvironmentalScan2021.pdf.

———. *Environmental Scan 2015.* Association of College and Research Libraries, March 2015. https://www.ala.org/acrl/sites/ala.org.acrl/files/content/publications/whitepapers/EnvironmentalScan15.pdf.

Allen, David. *Getting Things Done: The Art of Stress-Free Productivity.* Rev. ed. New York: Penguin, 2015.

Association of College and Research Libraries. *Standards for Libraries in Higher Education.* Association of College & Research Libraries, February 2018. https://www.ala.org/acrl/standards/standardslibraries.

Commission on Accrediting of the Association of Theological Schools. *2020 Standards of Accreditation.* The Association of Theological Schools, June 2020. https://www.ats.edu/files/galleries/standards-of-accreditation.pdf.

Heifetz, Ronald A., Alexander Grashow, and Martin Linsky. *The Practice of Adaptive Leadership: Tools and Tactics for Changing Your Organization and the World.* Boston: Harvard Business Press, 2009.

NN/LM NER Regional Advisory Council, Hospital Library Subcommittee. *Hospital Library Promotion Toolkit.* Network of the National Library of Medicine New England Region (NNLM NER) Repository, April 2007. https://doi.org/10.13028/YR5V-2J55.

Oliver Wight. *An Executive Guide to Integrated Business Planning.* Gloucester, UK: Oliver Wight EAME LLP, n.d. https://oliverwight-eame.com/resource/research/an-executive-guide-to-integrated-business-planning.

Sorensen, Dean. "Integrated Business Planning Is Not Just a Marketing Hoax." IndustryWeek, September 4, 2014. https://www.industryweek.com/software-systems/integrated-business-planning-not-just-marketing-hoax.

Wheatley, Margaret, and Deborah Frieze. *Walk Out Walk On: A Learning Journey into Communities Daring to Live the Future Now*. San Francisco: Berrett-Koehler, 2011.

Wheatley, Margaret J. *Leadership and the New Science: Discovering Order in a Chaotic World*. 3rd ed. San Francisco: Berrett-Koehler, 2006.

Whitney, Diana Kaplin, and Amanda Trosten-Bloom. *The Power of Appreciative Inquiry: A Practical Guide to Positive Change*. 2nd ed. San Francisco: Berrett-Koehler, 2010.

About the Author

Myka Kennedy Stephens is Seminary Librarian and Associate Professor of Theological Bibliography at Lancaster Theological Seminary in Lancaster, Pennsylvania. She provides oversight for theological library collections and services for Lancaster Theological Seminary and Moravian Theological Seminary, located in Bethlehem, Pennsylvania. Myka is also Founder and CEO of Fosgail, providing executive coaching and consulting services to professionals in libraries and related fields. She is fascinated by theories of human information behavior and their practical applications for library leadership and administration. She is also a strong advocate for open-source software for libraries and writes and presents widely on these topics. Myka holds degrees from Southern Methodist University (BA), Emory University (MDiv), and Florida State University (MSLIS), and she is a deaconess of The United Methodist Church appointed to service in librarianship.